YESTERDAY CALLING

WALTER HARRIS

Patagonia Press

YESTERDAY CALLING

Published by Patagonia Press

ISBN: 978-0-9928649-1-0

Author's website www.walterharris.co.uk

CD of interviews digitally remastered
by Ted Kendall
www.tedkendall.com

Cover Art by Angela Jane Swinn
www.angelajaneswinn.com

Printed and bound in Great Britain by
Berforts South West Ltd
www.berforts.co.uk

DEDICATION

To Alison

Not the light of my life so much as a galaxy.

Published novels by Walter Harris

GODHEAD

CLOVIS

THE MISTRESS OF DOWNING STREET

DROOP

THE DAY I DIED

THE FIFTH HORSEMAN

SALIVA

CREATURE FROM THE BLACK LAGOON
(WRITTEN AS CARL DREADSTONE, UK EDITION AS E.K. LEYTON)

WEREWOLF OF LONDON
(WRITTEN AS CARL DREADSTONE)

THE NEW AVENGERS: TO CATCH A RAT

AUTHOR'S NOTE

Ed Sullivan and American television came to pass at roughly the same time. Sullivan was the first major TV impresario. He was a large amiable man who wore a beautifully cut suit and a lugubrious smile. He was the first person I interviewed in my career as a broadcaster in New York in 1957. Had he not been amiable that career would probably not have happened, because the interview would have been a fiasco.

I reminded him of it a few years later, at a showbiz party at the Savoy. "You saved my life, Ed. I didn't know how to adjust the tape recorder properly, the atmospherics were the result of my fouling up and nothing to do with traffic interference, as you kindly suggested, and if you hadn't helped me by setting up the machine for me, I'd have been sunk."

He patted my shoulder and smiled. "I know," he said.

My memories of my career as a broadcaster came surging back a couple of years ago, when I decided to write *Yesterday Calling.* I was an independent, acredited to the Canadian Broadcasting Corporation and the BBC. This meant that I could choose my own interviewees, without having to submit all my ideas for subject matter to a producer, or use a studio for every broadcast, with the inevitable influence of the reactions of a studio audience.

Research into my now historical recordings indicated that the BBC had wiped nearly every tape after its use, whereas the CBC had placed them in its archives. There were thirty-nine altogether, including a walk with Gerald Durrell round his new Jersey Zoo, St.

Augrès with a background of posturing beasts and birds hand-reared at the zoo by Durrell himself.

My Family And Other Animals had been published some two years previously. These original recordings have been 'digitised' and may be played with the appropriate CD equipment.

CD PLAYLIST

1. Art Hodes (14th November 1904 in Russian Empire – 4th March 1993 in Harvey, Illinois), Arthur W. Hodes, known professionally as Art Hodes, was an American jazz and Speakeasy pianist. Hodes founded his own band in the 1940s and it would be associated with his home town of Chicago. He and his band played mostly in that area for the next forty years. He played with Sidney Bechet, Pee Wee Russell and many others.
Recording first broadcast CBC 24th April 1958.

2. Bea Lillie (29th May 1894 – 20th January 1989), Beatrice Gladys Lillie, known as Bea Lillie, was a Canadian-born British actress, singer and highly individualistic comedic performer. She began to perform as a child with her mother and sister. She made her West End debut in 1914 and soon gained notice in revues and light comedies, becoming known for her parodies of old-fashioned, flowery performing styles and absurd songs and sketches. She debuted in New York in 1924 and two years later starred in her first film, continuing to perform in both the US and UK. She was associated with the works of Noël Coward and Cole Porter. During World War II, Lillie was an inveterate entertainer of the troops. She won a Tony Award in 1953 for her revue An Evening With Beatrice Lillie.
Recording first broadcast CBC 17th November 1958.

3. Carnegie Hall. Probably the Front of House Manager; was personally hired by Andrew Carnegie himself in 1903.
Recording first broadcast CBC 12th November 1958.

4. Donald Campbell CBE (23rd March 1921 – 4th January 1967) was a British speed record breaker who broke eight absolute world speed records on water and on land in the 1950s and 1960s. He remains the only person to set both world land and water speed records in the same year (1964). He died during a speed attempt at the Lake District in northern England.

Interviewed with Bluebird at Goodwood shortly before becoming the first man to breach 400mph on land, at Utah, during his successful attempt on the world record.

CBC broadcast recording originally 26th August 1960.

5. Ed Sullivan (28th September 1901 – 13th October 1974) was an American TV impressario, sports and entertainment reporter, and longtime syndicated columnist for the New York Daily News and the Chicago Tribune New York News Syndicate. He is principally remembered as the creator and host of the television variety program The Toast of the Town, later popularly—and, eventually, officially—renamed The Ed Sullivan Show. Broadcast for 23 years from 1948 to 1971, it set a record as the longest-running variety show in US broadcast history. "It was, by almost any measure, the last great TV show," proclaimed television critic David Hinckley. "It's one of our fondest, dearest pop culture memories."

Interview conducted in New York.

Broadcast for first time by CBC 2nd May 1958.

6. John Wayne (born 26th May 1907 – 11th June 1979), also known by his nickname Duke, was an American actor and filmmaker. An Academy Award-winner for True Grit (1969), Wayne was among the top box office draws for three decades. Wayne's career took off in 1939, with John Ford's Stagecoach making him an instant star. He went on to star in 142 pictures. Biographer Ronald Davis said, "John

Wayne personified for millions the nation's frontier heritage. Eighty-three of his movies were Westerns, and in them he played cowboys, cavalrymen, and unconquerable loners extracted from the Republic's central creation myth. Wayne's other well-known Western roles include a cattleman driving his herd north on the Chisholm Trail in Red River (1948), a Civil War veteran whose young niece is abducted by a tribe of Comanches in The Searchers (1956), and a troubled rancher competing with a lawyer for a woman's hand in marriage in The Man Who Shot Liberty Valance (1962). He is also remembered for his roles in The Quiet Man (1952), Rio Bravo (1959), and The Longest Day (1962). In his final screen performance, he starred as an aging gunfighter battling cancer in The Shootist (1976).

Interviewed at the premier of The Alamo.

First CBC Broadcast 11th November 1960.

7. Sir Noël Coward (16th December 1899 – 26th March 1973) was an English playwright, composer, director, actor and singer, known for his wit, flamboyance, and what Time magazine called "a sense of personal style, a combination of cheek and chic, pose and poise". Many of his works, such as Hay Fever, Private Lives, Design for Living, Present Laughter and Blithe Spirit, have remained in the regular theatre repertoire. He composed hundreds of songs, in addition to well over a dozen musical theatre works (including the operetta Bitter Sweet and comic revues), screenplays, poetry, several volumes of short stories, the novel Pomp and Circumstance, and a three-volume autobiography. Coward's stage and film acting and directing career spanned six decades, during which he starred in many of his own works.

Recorded at Heathrow Airport. Broadcast CBC 15th November 1960

8. Phil Silvers (11th May 1911 – 1st November 1985) was an American entertainer and comedy actor, known as 'The King of Chutzpah'. He is best known for starring in The Phil Silvers Show, a 1950s sitcom set on a U.S. Army post in which he played Master Sergeant Ernest (Ernie) Bilko.
Broadcast CBC 2nd July 1959.

9. Siobhán McKenna (24th May 1923 – 16th November 1986) was an Irish stage and screen actress. Although primarily a stage actress, McKenna appeared in a number of made-for-television films and dramas. She also appeared in several motion pictures such as King of Kings in 1961, as the Virgin Mary. In 1964, she performed in Of Human Bondage and the following year in Doctor Zhivago. She also appeared in The Last Days of Pompeii (miniseries), as Fortunata, wife of Gaius(Laurence Olivier).
Broadcast CBC 20th October 1960.

10. Whitney Darrow Jr. (22nd August 1909 – 10th August 1999) was a prominent American cartoonist, who worked most of his career for The New Yorker, with some 1,500 of his cartoons printed in his nearly 50-year-long career with the magazine. The humour in Darrow's cartoons often focused on the absurdities and behavioural contradictions of middle-class suburban life, and featured characters such as judges, windbags, individuals in varying states of drunkenness, children and art.
CBC broadcast 29th October 1958.

11. Al Capp (28th September 1909 – 5th November 1979) was an American cartoonist and humourist best known for the satirical comic strip Li'l Abner, which he created in 1934 and continued writing and (with help from assistants) drawing until 1977. He also wrote the comic strips Abbie an' Slats (in the years 1937–45) and Long Sam (1954). He won the National Cartoonists Society's Reuben Award in 1947 for Cartoonist of the Year, and their 1979 Elzie Segar Award, posthumously for his 'unique and outstanding contribution to the profession of cartooning.' Comic strips dealt with northern urban experiences until the year Capp introduced 'Li'l Abner', the first strip based in the South. Although Capp was from Connecticut, he spent 43 years teaching the world about Dogpatch, reaching an estimated 60 million readers in over 900 American newspapers and 100 foreign papers in 28 countries.

Recorded in London in Savoy Hotel Press Bar 1958.

12. Danny Kaye (18th January 1911 – 3rd March 1987) was an American actor, singer, dancer, comedian, and musician. His performances featured physical comedy, idiosyncratic pantomimes, and rapid-fire novelty songs. Kaye starred in 17 movies, notably Wonder Man (1945), The Kid from Brooklyn (1946), The Secret Life of Walter Mitty (1947), The Inspector General (1949), Hans Christian Andersen (1952), White Christmas (1954), and The Court Jester (1956). He was the first ambassador-at-large of UNICEF in 1954 and received the French Legion of Honour in 1986 for his years of work with the organisation.

Recorded Dorchester Hotel London 1958.

13. Sophie Tucker (13th January 1887 – 9th February 1966) was an American singer, comedian, actress, and radio personality. Known for her stentorian delivery of comical and risqué songs, she was one of the most popular entertainers in America during the first half of the 20th century. She was widely known by the nickname 'The Last of the Red Hot Mamas'. In 1962, she performed in the Royal Variety Performance, which was also broadcast on the BBC. She appeared

on the Ed Sullivan Show on October 3rd 1965. For the colour broadcast, her last television appearance, she performed Give My Regards to Broadway, Louise, and her signature, Some Of These Days.
Interview recorded London 1958.

14. Gerald Durrell, OBE (7th January 1925 – 30th January 1995) was a British naturalist, zookeeper, conservationist, author and television presenter. He founded what are now called the Durrell Wildlife Conservation Trust and the Durrell Wildlife Park on the Channel Island of Jersey in 1959. He wrote a number of books based on his life as an animal collector and enthusiast. His family lived on Corfu until 1939. This interval was later the basis of the book My Family and Other Animals and its successors, Birds, Beasts, and Relatives and The Garden of the Gods, plus a few short stories such as My Donkey Sally. Durrell was home-schooled during this time by various family friends and private tutors, mostly friends of his eldest brother Lawrence (later to become a successful novelist).
Interviewed shortly after the inauguration of new zoo Les Augrès Manor, Jersey. Animals and birds participated in this recording, made in 1962.

The following tracks 15 - 19 were recorded in January 1960 at a private view of an exhibition of Stephen Ward's drawings at the Leggatt Brothers Gallery in Jermyn Street. Most of the guests had been sitters to Ward, a highly accomplished artist, the majority of those sitters were in politics and other forms of entertainment, most of whose clientele were members of Parliament and Society. He was awarded the exhibition by the Leggatt Brothers because he had saved Hugh Leggatt's life through his skills as an osteopath when Leggatt fell off a horse and was told by specialists that his neck was broken, and beyond cure. Other sitters at the exhibition whom Harris recorded were the socialite Nubar Gulbenkian, Tufton Beamish (who confides during the interview that he would have voted for Nixon rather than Kennedy, as his wife was an American republican and would have never have forgiven him), Lord Robert Boothby (who had been for years the lover of Lady Dorothy, the Prime Minister's wife, and after his death was found guilty of perjury and pederasty with the rent boys he shared with the gangster, Ronnie Kray), and the senior prosecutor at the Nazi War Crimes Trials at Nuremberg, Lord William (previously Sir Hartley) Shawcross.

15. Nubar Sarkis Gulbenkian (2nd June 1896 – 10th January 1972) was an Armenian business magnate and socialite born in the Ottoman empire. A Society eccentric, Nubar was the son of Calouste Gulbenkian, popularly known as 'Mr 5%'. His nickname derived from the cut he received from Middle East oil company deals.

16. Robert Boothby, Baron Boothby, KBE (12th February 1900 – 16th July 1986), often known as Bob Boothby, was a British Conservative politician. From 1930 he had a long affair with Lady Dorothy Macmillan, wife of the Conservative politician Harold Macmillan (who would serve as prime minister from 1957 until 1963). In 1963 Boothby began an illicit affair with East End cat burglar Leslie Holt (d. 1979), a younger man he met at a gambling club. Holt introduced him to the gangster Ronald Kray, the younger Kray twin, who (allegedly) supplied Boothby with young men and arranged orgies in Cedra Court, receiving personal favours from Boothby in return. After his death, Boothby was found guilty of sodomy and perjury.

17. William Shawcross, Baron Shawcross, GBE, PC, QC (4th February 1902 – 10th July 2003), known from 1945 to 1959 as Sir Hartley Shawcross, was a British barrister and politician and the lead British prosecutor at the Nuremberg War Crimes tribunal. Shawcross's advocacy was instrumental in obtaining convictions against the remaining Nazi leadership, on grounds which were perceived as fair and lawful. In 1961 he was appointed the chairman of the second Royal Commission on the Press. In 1967 he became one of the directors of The Times responsible for ensuring its editorial independence. He resigned on being appointed chairman of the Press Council in 1974. From 1974 to 1978 he was chairman of the Press Council.

18. Tufton Victor Hamilton Beamish, Baron Chelwood, MC, DL (27th January 1917 – 6th April 1989) was a British Army officer, Conservative Party Member of Parliament for Lewes (1945–1974), and author. During the Second World War, he served in France, Belgium (1940), Malaya (1942), India and Burma (1942–43), North Africa and Italy (1943–44). In 1940 he was awarded the Military Cross; was knighted in 1961 and upon his retirement from the House of Commons was created a life peer as Baron Chelwood, of Lewes in May 1974. He was one of that school of MPs which hated staying in the House and liked to get out and about.

19. Stephen Ward (19th October 1912 – 3rd August 1963) was an English osteopath and artist who was one of the central figures in the 1963 Profumo Affair, a British political scandal which brought about the resignation of John Profumo, the Secretary of State for War, and contributed to the defeat of the Conservative government a year later. Ward was abandoned by his society friends and exposed to the contempt and hostility of prosecuting counsel and judge. Despite the relative paucity of evidence and the dismissal of most of the charges against him, he was convicted on two counts of living off immoral earnings. However, before the verdict was announced, Ward took an overdose of sleeping pills and died three days later.

The present recording is the only known recording of Stephen Ward.

PRELUDE

The history of recorded sound is quite brief; it was only in 1880 that the American inventor Thomas Edison was able to record by means of electrical impulses activated by sound and directed onto a cylinder whose principal constituent was silver paper.

Edison called the machine a phonograph, and hoped that the cylinder carrying the message would qualify as a parcel rather than a letter, which was much more expensive to send.

However, not only were the cylinders highly frangible and the voice transmissions smothered by acoustic disturbance, the postal authorities turned down the idea that they could be sent as parcel post. Edison decided therefore to concentrate on more profitable and practical inventions, such as the telegraph and light bulb, but did mention the phonograph at a press conference he held whilst on a visit to London.

One of the people attending the conference was a cavalry colonel during the Civil War. His name was George Edward Gouraud, and his valour won him America's highest decoration, the Congressional Medal of Honour.

After a brief period in the Customs service, Gouraud joined George Pullman, inventor of the sleeping car, in order to market the cars in Europe. On meeting Edison and learning about the phonograph, Gouraud became an apostle of the machine and determined to help Edison perfect it. He left Pullman and went back to America with Edison, his ambition to sell the phonograph strongly ignited. It was a unique means of communication, he insisted, and he intended to stand at the inventor's shoulder until he had carried out the necessary development of the machine and its cylinders.

Almost forcibly, he persuaded Edison to return to the phonograph until he found a solution to its drawbacks and could offer it the future the colonel had started to foresee for it.

It took nearly two years before a revised and greatly improved phonograph with hardier cylinders made mainly of wax was ready.

In 1887 Gouraud crossed the Atlantic again with a small cargo of the appliances and a highly ambitious marketing strategy. His intention was to interview a hundred eminent Victorians, hopefully including the Queen herself.

Gouraud's favourite technique was to invite an interviewee to dinner, relax him with a sufficiency of wine and present him with the recording aperture of the phonograph comfortably within reach of his mouth. Usually the colonel would start the recording with a personal message to Edison saying something such as:"Edison, listen to this. It's Sir Arthur Sullivan."

Sullivan in fact did not look benevolently on the phonograph. Interviewed after the First Night of *Yeoman of the Guard* the composer growled that future generations would be cursed by having to listen to 'the sort of dreadful rendition of his music rendered by the appliance'.

One of the phonograph's more bizarre triumphs was when Otto von Bismarck was persuaded to record a cowboy song in English, thus outraging his family, who were apparently scandalised by the Iron Chancellor's behaviour, but to be interviewed by Gouraud had become fashionable.

By the time he died in 1912 Gouraud had played a major part in helping transform Edison's phonograph into a machine which reliably lifted professional voices out of opera and concert halls and off the stage into peoples' own homes for them to enjoy.

In the same year, Marconi brought his invention of wireless to fruition and John Reith, destined to be the BBC's first Director-General, reached the age of twenty-one.

He had been born in July 1889 and in 1922, as general manager of the Corporation and later Director-General, would start to cast his influence across the world.

The Phonograph would place the broadcast material permanently on record.

YESTERDAY CALLING

CHAPTER ONE

As it happened, my first interviewee should have been the poet Ezra Pound, who escaped being executed for treason just after the Second World War, because of the doubts of some members of Congress and the United States Supreme Court concerning his origins, as well as his sanity.

Unlike the British, who had had no hesitation in executing Sir Roger Casement for treason during the Great War, even though he was born in the Republic of Ireland, these American politicians and legislators argued that if, as they suspected, Pound had been born in Canada, he could hardly be executed for treason against the United States.

After much argument and ill-temper, it was decided by the relevant authorities that Ezra Pound had acted as he had because he was mad, and he was therefore sentenced to be incarcerated indefinitely in St Elizabeth's Hospital for the Criminally Insane, just across the Virginian State Line from Washington D C.

William Joyce, an Irishman who, like Pound, resorted to radio to commit treason, was not so lucky; captured at the end of the Second World War, he was promptly hanged as a traitor at London's Wandsworth Prison by the British authorities.

The technique used by the two men was quite different: Joyce had a high-pitched, sneering voice which earned him the nickname Lord Haw Haw, and often discomfited his British audience, though they laughed at him, by broadcasting some local detail such as that the town hall clock in some English market town was three minutes slow.

1

This implied that moles, known as Fifth Columnists, or German spies landed from U-boats, were actively sending accurate information back to Berlin. It was far more likely that such information came from casual Luftwaffe reconnaissance aircraft.

Pound's broadcasts emanated from Rome, and were aimed principally at deflecting the powerful sense of purpose of the American military, especially General Mark Clark's Sixth Army advancing up through the centre of Italy. Pound tried to persuade the troops that whilst they were risking their lives overseas in battle, their wives and girl friends were under siege, and gladly surrendering to an army of seducers.

Pound's was a classic case of a poet not being appreciated in his own country, and I was sufficiently intrigued by it to seek an interview with him in 1958 on behalf of the Canadian Broadcasting Corporation, to which I had recently been accredited as an independent broadcaster.

Apparently born in Idaho, in spite of the post-war rumours about his being a Canadian, Pound had become Professor of Romance Languages at Wabash Presbyterian College in Pennsylvania when he was only twenty-two. He wrote poetry but could not get it published.

Enraged by the obtuseness of those who, he thought, refused to accept his obvious genius, he decided in mid-term to throw such possessions as he had into a suitcase and set sail for Italy, where he made his home in Venice, paying for the publication of his first book of poems and at last tasting success.

Instead of returning to America, therefore, he completed his allegiance to Italy by remaining there, and added to his distinction as a poet by becoming a critic of art and sculpture. In the 20s he befriended Ernest Hemingway and helped James Joyce financially, as well as praising and encouraging T.S. Eliot with the writing of *The Love Song of J. Alfred Prufrock* and *The Wasteland*.

In 1924 Pound decided to live permanently in Rapallo. Early in life he had fallen under the influence of a Canadian called Douglas, who had founded the fascistic Canadian Social Credit Party (Socred), hence perhaps the confusion about his nationality.

Benito Mussolini had come to power in Italy two years before Pound's Rapallo move, which made the poet feel even more at home there. When America entered the war he decided once more to continue to make his home in Italy rather than return to America.

At the end of the War, captured and charged with being a traitor, Pound was kept in a cage made of runway matting at Rome's Ciampino Airport for six weeks, and after that for six months in a prison camp in Pisa, where he employed his time translating Confucius into English and starting work on his poem *The Pisan Cantos*.

When I telephoned St Elizabeth's and, through Superintendent Oberholtzer, who ran the place, made an appointment for a meeting with Ezra Pound, he had been incarcerated for approximately nine years.

In order to make an early start, I spent the night before my visit at Washington's Jefferson Hotel, where in the bar I recognised two senators often in the news, Mike Mansfield, Leader of the Committee for Foreign Affairs, and Senator John McLellan of Arkansas, the newly appointed Chairman of the Senate Government Operations Committee, popularly known as the Senate Racketbusting Committee. They were charged with giving gangsters, principally the Mafia, a much tougher time than they had been having. Mansfield left, and MacLellan caught my eye.

"Good evening," he said.

"Good evening, Senator."

He smiled at my acknowledging who he was. "You're from the United Kingdom?"

3

I told him I was from London.

"Are you interested in baseball?"

I told him I hadn't seen enough of it to be sure.

"Well I'm going upstairs to watch a game now. If you want to come with me, we can chat during the commercials." We went to his room and sat on the edge of the bed and I waited impatiently for the commercials so that we could discuss gangsters.

However, during the break from the action the phone rang and the caller was J Edgar Hoover. MacLellan signalled that it was a private call so I excused myself and went back to my room. Later that night the Senator was called to an emergency meeting with Hoover and other members of the FBI and, according to the New York Times the following day, briefed about a major raid the Bureau was carrying out on an army of mafiosi which had assembled for a series of Family gatherings in the foothills of the Appalachian Mountains just outside New York.

The FBI broke up the meetings and chased the godfathers out of the area, arresting some of them and spreading a fair degree of humiliation. One of the most senior mafiosi, Frank Costello, was shot in the head but not fatally, and some time later the Sicillian gangster 'Lucky' Luciano's principal enforcer, Alberto Anastasia, was shot and killed by his opposite number in another gang whilst having a shave in a Sixth Avenue barber's shop, near Carnegie Hall.

It wasn't long before the Senator for Arkansas became a household name in America.

I arrived at St Elizabeth's at nine a.m. as arranged. Initially I thought the hospital resembled a large country hotel as we approached it up a wide driveway. Some people ambled along paths through well-cut grass, and there were cordial waves from others standing on verandas whose windows glittered in the rays of the rising sun. It was at that point I realised the verandas were behind metal bars running from ceiling to floor, and that the people standing on them were not waving but gesticulating

I noticed that others, those making their way along the paths, were either walking aimlessly, or with a brisk sense of purpose which often abruptly evaporated, leaving them to come to a vacant-eyed halt.

The taxi turned in to stop in front of reception, and I asked the driver to wait whilst I had a word with the Superintendent. He arrived through an inner door into the lobby as soon as a telephonist had announced me, and held out his hand.

"Good morning, Mr. Harris," he greeted me, with the sort of amiability that means bad news. "Nice to see you. I'm sorry to say Ezra's not here."

"Oh. When will he back?"

"He won't be. At least not as a patient. The order for his immediate release came in yesterday afternoon. Frankly, I never thought there was anything the matter with his mind, but I gave the impression when I addressed the Congressional Committee that I thought he was insane because otherwise he would probably have wound up in the electric chair. One of those strange contradictions. At least if I could get to look after him, his life here would be quite tolerable, and he'd likely get out one day."

"My day," I couldn't help saying. "He's been here nine years and I've missed him by half an hour."

He shrugged. "That's the way it sometimes goes, I guess."

"Anyway, thank you for setting up our meeting in the first place."

He put his large head on one side. "I'm sorry it didn't work out, Mr. Harris. "Tell you what I'll do, though. I'll tell you where he is."

"Really? That would be marvellous."

"Well, I realise it's a tough break for you to come out here all hyped up for the interview and find him gone. Just don't broadcast the fact I've passed on privileged information." He chuckled.

"He's gone to a safe house in Brothers Road. It's a few miles from here, brand new neighbourhood, haven't even laid the turf yet. Just a desert but the plumbing and electricity are in. Someone picked him up in a red and white small car, a Nash Metropolitan. It'll likely be outside the house, as they haven't finished laying the driveway yet."

I thanked him, and he told me it was, in the circumstances, the least he could do. We shook hands warmly. "By the way, have you ever read any of Pound's poetry?" I asked.

"Can't say I have. I did try, but I'm a simple man, and I found it way too complex. In fact, if anything was going to prove he was insane, I'd say it was what he wrote, but then I'm no critic."

Brothers Road was empty of parked cars except for one, a red and white Nash Metropolitan. We pulled up in front of it and I wrestled with my Ampex tape recorder, which was in the form of two fairly heavy suitcases. I hefted them and carried them up the steps where I thankfully put them down on the stoop and rang the bell at the side of the aluminium screen door.

The room beyond was frugally furnished, empty except for an occasional table or two and a couple of chairs. A small vase of flowers lent a touch of incongruous colour to the seemingly uninhabited house stuck in its Saharan surroundings.

A short, skinny woman came into the room, saw me peering through the screen door, and without hesitation charged at me like a buffalo from behind a thorn bush.

I reacted by stepping backwards and losing my footing, which apparently satisfied her, as she didn't follow me. I lay on my back in the dusty road and the taxi driver, a large young Virginian, grinned down at me.

"Ah sure wish Ah had a camera with me," he drawled, leaning forward to help me up, "then Ah could take a photograph of you lyin' there and say the Pounds had throwed you out."

At least the Ampex as well as myself had survived more or less intact, so chuckling to himself for most of the way the driver took me back to the Jefferson, where I picked up my hire car and drove on to New York.

CHAPTER TWO

Although I had always had the idea of eventually basing myself in New York, I chose to go to Canada first, partly to acclimatise myself to North America, and partly because I had been sponsored by a Canadian company to do a series of broadcasts featuring dance music and jazz during my first migration, to Brazil, which I have written about in another book. The trouble was that when, after five years, I felt the urge to leave Brazil and head north, thanks to a substantial Brazilian currency devaluation just before I left and my fondness for living further up the scale than I could really afford, I arrived in Montreal broke.

Instead of staying, as friends in Brazil had originally suggested, at the city's finest hotel, the Ritz Carlton, I found myself working in its kitchens at night as assistant to a dumbwaiter, putting hot plates of food into a tiny lift which scuttled up the shaft to be collected by someone from room service. Later the plates came down, usually with a generous residue of congealing food which went into the kitchen waste bins or was fed to some favoured local dogs.

I arrived in Montreal in April 1953, and stayed at an egregious Green Street lodging house, in the Mount Royal area. Green Street was a narrow, skinny thoroughfare, and my new abode possessed a slightly sinister quality. The house was built round a large well off which various rooms opened, including the bathroom. One of the tenants, an elderly French Canadian who resembled a film version of Dickens's Miss Haversham, had a habit of sleep-walking late at night from her room to the bathroom, sitting on the loo with the door open, and uttering a series of moans which increased in volume until she sounded like Lady Macbeth trying to wash a couple of gallons of blood off her hands.

"Mon Dieu mon Dieu mon Dieu!" she wailed repeatedly and more and more loudly, but added nothing further in the way of prayers. Apparently calling God's name was sufficient; she had nothing to ask of Him.

Nobody went to comfort her or try to shut her up; I suppose they were used to her, but her evident misery was upsetting.

Next door to the house was a shop selling TV sets, offering passers-by free entertainment. I remember standing outside it for more than an hour, watching the Coronation taking place in Westminster Abbey whilst the rain poured down in both London and Montreal.

After that I went on to my daytime job, selling folding doors in Outremont, one of the French quarters of the city.

This was a job which caused me considerable apprehension, owing to my complete lack of manual dexterity. The doors were constructed of aluminium trellis under an insect-proof plastic material, and had to fit perfectly into their allotted space. That required the ability to measure the door and doorway with absolute accuracy; there was no question of some sort of Procrustean adjustment. If the door was either too wide or too narrow, there was nothing for it but to scrap it, and they were expensive.

Furthermore, the French spoken in Canada is more akin to Norman French than the Parisian version of the language taught in England, and the French Canadians are proud of its incomprehensibility. Taking down the householder's dictation regarding requirements meant a good deal of concentration; guesswork was impossible.

The door company's offices, however, taught me a lot about Canadian geography. The walls were covered in maps of the country's provinces and cities and, as in Brazil, many of them had received their names historically from native Indian tribes: Ottawa; Chicotimi; Manitoba; Saskatchewan; Shuswap.

There was also of course Moose Jaw, whose name demanded a visit, but I never found the time to go.

I had visited the Canadian Broadcasting Corporation's Offices in Montreal, but was advised that as an Anglophone I should go to their Toronto offices if I wanted a job as a broadcaster, so I decided to move on to Toronto as soon as I wrecked a folding door, which happened during my second week in the field.

Thanks to my working hours and the Green Street sleep-walker I had had very little sleep in Montreal; the first thing I intended to do in Toronto was to buy a paper, stay awake long enough to read the relevant classified ads, find a decent lodging house and sleep the clock round.

The place I found was on Jarvis Street, which runs from the northern sector of Toronto south towards Lake Ontario and parallel with the well-known avenue Bay Street. The landlord was called Ennis Rose, and I suspected him at once of being a materialist masquerading as a visionary. I think he held peculiar religious beliefs, but then as far as I am concerned they all are. Whatever his beliefs were, there was something of the bishop about him; he smelled purple.

At meal times especially, he took on the hue of an evangelist, uttering grace with fervour, his arms wide and his vocal chords locked in a liturgical cadence which reminded me of a Rogers and Hart song called Johnny One-Note.

Most of those sitting at table were young Canadian men from different parts of the country, several married and with very young children. They had come to Toronto to prospect for career opportunities and were missing their families. One, George Hellman,

10

was the son of Finnish immigrants who had come to Canada to escape the Soviet invasion threat to their country. George was to do very well, running a private radio station, and became a close friend of mine. When I returned to England we phoned each other several times a year, a process which in those days was tedious and required an operator and often several hours of waiting.

The last time I called him from London was on a Saturday morning. I had originally planned to talk to him the next day, but for some reason changed my mind.

He was at his home in Port Credit, at that time more of a village than a town, between Toronto and Niagara. We spoke for about ten minutes about a trip I was shortly going to make to Canada with my son Julian. The three of us would then drive through the Rockies.

George's wife rang me a few days later. She was sobbing. "George just died. You were the last person he ever spoke to, Walter," she told me. "After he hung up from talking to you he went into the garden, where he liked to sit on the swing sometimes because he said it helped him think.

"He'd been there a few minutes when he called me and I hurried to him because of the way he sounded, sort of frightened, but I was too late. He died just as I got to him."

I was in shock and wanted to put my arms round her, but she was three thousand miles away. I was glad I hadn't waited till the Sunday to call him. It was thirty years to the day since we had first met at Ennis's.

CHAPTER THREE

The top end of Jarvis Street basked in the sunshine of the Presbyterian respectability to which Toronto was prone; halfway down, beyond my new digs, were the studios and offices of CBC.

Not much further in the direction of Lake Ontario, Jarvis Street began to let its hair down, proffering several pubs in which men and women were severely segregated, and an extremely raffish hotel, called simply The Jarvis Hotel, where they were encouraged to join together.

It took me some time to get used to the drinking laws of those days. There were bars where men and women could sit down together, provided they arrived together. Nobody except the waiters was allowed to carry a drink from the bar to the customer's table, and it was forbidden to stand whilst drinking.

The only bar in the city exempt from these rules was Maloney's Art Gallery - I have no idea why.

As for buying a bottle of spirits or a case of lager at an off-licence, the would-be customer was subjected to extremes of bureaucratically-induced stress. This began with a drive to an out-of-town warehouse, whose interior decorations were invariably prison green.

The first person the customer had to defer to was not a warder but a clerk standing behind a wooden bar whose perimeter ran for a hundred yards or so to a cubby-hole resembling a confessional. Within sat a sacerdotal and sombre creature, who confronted the supplicant with a list of beverage names and prices per case mentioned in a tone of voice appropriate for reciting sins and imposing Hail Marys.

Having ticked the details of the desired alcohol, the sinner was moved on towards another confessional, this time containing a pair of chipmunk people, who chattered and squealed at each other in a haze of thin laughter before turning to the customer, scrutinising the list and calculating the payment due.

After payment a receipt was issued, and the last Long March, to the Delivery Point, resulted in the appearance of the order, which was handed over reluctantly, as if some vital detail of the transaction had been overlooked and needed to be double-checked. I can't remember if there was a limit on the number of bottles of alcoholic beverages one was permitted to buy at each visit; certainly it took some time, and a generous contribution from the newly acquired purchase, to recover from the experience.

CHAPTER FOUR

I reconnoitred the chances of employment at CBC as soon as I had moved into my lodgings. Nobody seemed very interested in talking to me about any sort of broadcasting job. Someone hinted that I might find things easier if I changed my English accent.

I confided my difficulties to Elizabeth Cleaton, one of the receptionists at CBC who was also English and a Londoner. She was as thin as a razor blade and viewed sideways on became almost invisible, but she had a warm if slightly fussy persona, and a ballet background which she hoped to translate into a television series for the Corporation on how to dance Swan Lake.

"At the present moment there's a good deal of politics here," she told me. "The people who aren't very bright have taken over from the people who are. I don't think they'll be in power for much longer, though. If you take a tip from me, go and have a drink at about midday at the Queen's Head, just down Jarvis on the opposite side to us. There'll probably be a big Irish-Canadian sitting there with a pint or two in front of him. His name's Harry Boyle and he's the brightest of the lot. Officially he's Chairman of CBC for Ontario, but his power's been slowly siphoned away.

"He was recently promoted downwards, as he puts it, but you could do worse than have a drink with him."

I thanked her and she and I arranged to meet at Maloney's the following evening.

The Queen's Head looked as though its signboard had been newly-painted, with a portrait of Elizabeth the Second that made her seem like a schoolgirl under her crown. The sign directly contradicted the pub's interior, gloomy as an undertaker's with beer

14

smelling of embalming fluid. There was only one man in the men's section, with yellowish hair and a large face. He looked up as I came in and greeted him and asked if he was Harry Boyle. He scrutinised me, good morning'd me in return, and said he was. I asked if I could sit at his table and he pointed to a chair.

"Beer?" I nodded and thanked him and the waiter brought me one, put it on the table and went back to the bar. "My name's Walter Harris," I said.

"English by the sound of you."

"Yes. I was told by an English CBC receptionist called Elizabeth Cleaton that you might be here." I told him what Elizabeth had said about him, and he laughed.

"What field of broadcasting are you interested in?"

I gave him my brief resumé and added that I would like to be an interviewer and also a writer, for radio.

"You seem to have self-confidence. That's probably as useful as talent. In fact, I suppose it *is* a talent." He smiled. "In my experience, English interviewers tend by and large to be too deferential and to confuse deference with courtesy. I think if they could hear themselves they'd be horrified at the extent of their humility, which is an interviewer's blight. It makes them all sound like Squeers.

"An interviewer needs to be in charge of the interview but maintain his authority as unassumingly as possible. The subtlest interviewers, like the subtlest wives, lead from behind—you're not in the business of showing how clever you are.

"If you're interviewing a politician, for instance, listen to his answers and remember that, although in life one should try to keep things simple, it's not always possible to do that. Respect his complexity—politics is a complex trade. Would you like another beer?"

"Thank you. May I have a Molsom's?"

15

Harry signalled a waiter and gave the order. "I didn't mean to give you a training course in interviewing over a drink, but if you remember what I've told you, you won't go far wrong. And never forget whose voice the public wants to concentrate on—the one that's answering the questions, not the one that's putting them."

I thanked him, and he got up to leave. "Come here tomorrow at the same time, if you like. And ask Elizabeth to tell you if anything's going on I ought to know about."

"Of course." We shook hands and I drank the bottle of Molsom's and watched Harry's broad back as he went back up Jarvis Street's gentle but attenuated gradient. I felt what might be a dangerous surge of encouragement; the Ezra Pound incident had taught me that no deal is ever done till it's signed.

The next day, I entered the sepulchral precincts of the Queen's Head shortly before noon. Harry was sitting at the same table as before; I was to find out that he never sat anywhere else. It was beside a window, and from his perspective had a good view of Jarvis Street and its restless traffic. I waved to him and went to the bar, where I ordered another drink for Harry and a Molsom's for myself. The same waiter who had served us the previous day brought the glasses on a small tray and Harry raised his in a silent toast.

"The rats are still in possession of the ship." He gestured in the direction of the CBC buildings. "I hope you have a chance one day to take some of the advice about interviewing which I gave you yesterday, but it's your immediate survival that should take priority.

"So take a job: doesn't have to be anything grand, just something that'll pay a living wage and give you enough time to keep your eyes open till you find one you think has a future. I can't guarantee you one as yet and I have no idea how long it will be before that might happen.

16

"You've been a reporter; try the Toronto Star and the Toronto Globe and Mail, whose editor is a Scot—as you might guess—called Hamish McGeachy.

"We've also got some major advertising companies here in Toronto—Cockfield Brown and MacLaren's are two you might think of selling yourself to. CBC could probably find you a night job, like cleaning film. It's a humble enough job, threading film on a spool through a tank of carbon tetrachloride, but it'll keep you in Molsom's and beef sandwiches.

"If I can I'll help you, because I think you're worth giving a chance to, but at the moment I get a decent pay packet with no power to go with it, like a constitutional monarch. CBC doesn't need a constitutional monarch; what it needs is a street fighter with a good brain that's still intact."

"I'm grateful for the advice, Harry. Do you have any idea at all how long it'll be before you're back in business?"

He gave a grim smile. "If I have my way, yesterday," he answered. "I'm as uncertain in a way as you are about what's going to happen next. Now I'm going back to my office, and I suggest you set about right away finding an office to go back to yourself."

He pushed his chair back. "I'll be here Wednesday next week. Keep me posted on how you're doing."

"I will. Thank you, Harry." He waved and went out, and I made my way back to Ennis's. My landord's sonorous tones were audible before I reached the dining-room. I decided they were the last thing I wanted to hear at that moment, turned about, and left the house without eating. The ecclesiastical smell of purple was overwhelming.

By the time I arrived at Maloney's that evening, I was starving, but at least I had a job: MacLaren's had taken me on probation as a trainee copywriter. My salary was quite generous, my hours of work short. "We're paying for your imagination," they told me. "That

17

doesn't mean simply changing the order of 'marvellous' and 'amazing' in an advertisement. And you must learn to differentiate between an ad that entertains but doesn't sell, and an ad that sells and maybe does both, but selling's more important."

Apparently one of the best ads ever to arrive on a poster was the one showing a baby buggy, as prams were called in Canada and the US, with the caption: The Only Convertible to Out-Sell Ford. It failed, however, to have much impact on the sale of Fords, and was not displayed for long, which seemed a great pity.

Elizabeth had dressed up for our date. Her hair had been professionally coiffed and her rather small eyes extended by a make-up whose shade I couldn't quite make out in Maloney's twilight, arranged more for romance than cosmetic analysis.

I told her my news and she showed an appropriate degree of excitement. "Marvellous, jolly well done! People usually have to wait ages to get a job like that!"

Gambling that I could persuade MacLaren's to advance me enough for the rent, I ordered a bottle of Taittainger and glasses, and had the pleasure of carrying them to our table myself. Later, we had an excellent meal, but I couldn't take Elizabeth back to Jarvis Street because Ennis seemed to have a Jezebel complex about all girls and relentlessly quarantined his male guests against them.

It was nearly the end of August so Elizabeth and I decided, as the songwriters Harry Warren and Al Dubin put it, to shuffle off to Buffalo for, as it turned out, the worst weekend of our lives.

What we had forgotten was that September 1st was Labour Day, and America was on the move. We had decided to travel to Buffalo by train, not knowing that the town has arguably the longest street in the world, Delaware Avenue, and that we were destined to walk the length of it.

There were no taxis available, the buses were packed, and mercifully I can't remember how far we walked in search of somewhere to stay—the hotels were full and one could have built a bonfire big enough to burn an army of martyrs from the dozens of 'no vacancy' signs that spattered the windows of every building. I think we gave up when we reached a house with a number in the seventeen thousands.

At last we reached a dwelling where was a 'vacancy' sign in the window, and assumed the owner had forgotten to remove it, but there was indeed a room that was free.

Feeling like a witch's familiar, I followed the hag who opened the front door up a flight of stairs to a door sticky with varnish. The floor too, seemed reluctant to release anyone who stood on it—I was beginning to feel like a fly mortally marooned in a pitcher plant.

"The last gennelman who took this room stayed two years before he die—moved away" our guide and helper told us, opening the door with a rusty key big enough for a dungeon. It shrieked as it entered the lock. The room was tiny, and its only window framed a brick wall about a foot away.

I looked at Elizabeth, who sank on to the bed. "We'll take it," I said.

"It's a nice room, you won't regret it."

We were too exhausted to argue. We drew the curtain to hide the looming wall, and slept.

I don't think either of us ever shuffled off to Buffalo again.

My job at MacLaren's ended within six weeks of my starting there. One of the agency's biggest accounts was Esso gasoline, which had originally been one of the forty or so Standard Oil companies owned by John D Rockefeller.

In 1953 Esso brought out a new mark of gasoline called Esso X, but as a copywriter I couldn't keep my sense of the ridiculous in check. I suggested that we change the copy from: 'Next time you fill up, ask for Esso X' to a poster urging: 'Next time you fill up, shout SOB!' (Son of a Bitch!) which was a far ruder oath in Canada and America than in England.

I hoped for consolation and understanding from Elizabeth, who however was unsympathetic. "Why do you have to be such an idiot?" She did however accept a dinner invitation on the evening of the day I was fired, and I decided to push the boat out and not worry till the following day about where the next boat was going to come from.

When I arrived at her house, she was not in, and the small gardens belonging to it and the one next door were already covered by thickly-falling snow. Although I was wearing a thick overcoat, I felt chilled, especially round the feet.

After half an hour or so, Elizabeth arrived, but she was not alone. "This is Charles Leggatt," she told me. "Charles, this is, er, oh dear, I can't remember his name!" I had no intention of enlightening her. "Well, you haven't seen me since we got up this morning," I said ungallantly. "You were, I thought, coming out to dinner with me tonight! Now you turn up with a complete stranger and forget my name! You'd better make up your mind!"

"Don't you think you're being rather immature?" Leggatt's voice was very English, and had an inbuilt sneer. I lost my temper, raised my arm in its heavy, damp overcoat sleeve, and aimed a punch at him. He was standing between Elizabeth and myself, and ducked, so the punch landed on her jaw. It was the greatest compliment I could have paid her. I had shown my love, my passion for her, I had been prepared to joust to win her, I was her knight!

Leggatt rather spoiled things by deciding not to try to hit me back. He had obviously come to the conclusion that a woman who suffered from amnesia when it came to her lover's name but whose memory was fully restored when introducing a complete stranger, wasn't worth fighting over.

"Your spectacles landed in the garden next door," he told me, ignoring her. "I'd better help you find them." The two of us went into the garden and prodded about till Leggatt spotted them and picked them up.

"Thank you." I almost called him Charles in the warm spirit of masculine amity which had so swiftly, if improbably, united us.

"My pleasure. In the circumstances, perhaps I'd better push off."

He trudged out of the gate and down the road. Elizabeth threw her arms round me.

"Never mind, darling, you didn't mean to hurt me." Her eyes were shining, as if I had committed an act of heroism instead of almost knocking her out. "Let me straighten them."

"Thank you." I handed her the twisted frame. A lens fell out as she handed it back. I couldn't see anything, but I appreciated the gesture. She took my arm and led me to the gate. "Let's go to dinner," she said, "it's on me."

Not long afterwards, she returned to England to comfort her mother, who had been diagnosed as suffering from a disease of the scalp called Alopecia Areata, which causes hair loss. She went bald and had to sleep in a beret, thus driving away her lover. Both of them were constantly consoled by Elizabeth in an effort to bring them together again; so far as I remember her mother's hair finally returned, but her lover didn't.

I decided to go back to selling the Encyclopaedia Britannica, at which I had been quite successful in Rio and São Paulo during my Brazilian period, before I started my dance music programmes.

After going to see several prospective clients with my sales kit, I found myself with a book publisher. I can remember his appearance, but not his first name, perhaps because my memory switches off as

21

soon as his soft voice and black-rimmed spectacles embedded in an aureole of silver hair come to mind. I will call him by his surname of Donohue; he was not a first name man.

"Do you enjoy selling the Britannica, Mr Harris?" he asked me.

I told him I did.

"I reckon if you can sell that you can sell pretty well anything?"

"It's not too difficult to sell any product as long as you believe in it. With the possible exception of Christianity," I couldn't refrain from adding. I tried to coax a smile from his set mouth. "It's when you have no belief in your product that things become more difficult."

"How about coffee?" For a moment I thought he was offering me a cup.

"Coffee?"

"Vending machines, I believe they're going to be a big deal. I've been looking for a partner for a vending machine project. In fact, I've bought a vending machine round, sited in offices and one or two cinemas. Are you interested?"

"Well, I know nothing at all about the business."

"You're young. You'll soon learn. Do you have a car?"

"Not yet."

"I'll get you one. You'll need to be able to transport replenishments for the machines each day—coffee, dried milk powder, sugar and so forth."

"What about salary?" I asked.

"You don't get a salary; as a partner, you get a share of the profits." That turned out to be such a disingenuous answer it took me a long time ever again to trust well-dressed men with silver hair and black-rimmed glasses.

"Supposing there aren't any profits to share?"

"Then you'll have failed at the job." He smiled. "And I shall have to find another partner or write off my investment. Why not try it and see how you get on?"

"I'll still need some income."

"The books I've looked at suggest that the machines are currently taking enough cash to enable you to make a living."

"That means I'll be rattling about with pockets filled with dimes and quarters."

"You'll be able to change them for paper money at the bank every day."

It would be something to occupy me until Harry's political fortunes changed. I might even be successful. And of course there was the promised car.

"I'll have a go," I said.

"Good. Come round at noon tomorrow and I'll give you a list of the coffee sites and suppliers. We can discuss details about the company, what we're going to call it, setting up a bank account and so forth, after lunch."

We shook hands on the deal, and I left him at his handsome walnut desk, surrounded by shelves of paperbacks and volumes bound in morocco leather, and stepped out into the bitter afternoon. Instinct told me not to get too excited by my impending career swerve. I hoped Harry wouldn't regard it as a disqualification for the job I really wanted. At least, I suspected, it would make him laugh.

The meeting with Donohue the following afternoon ended with his handing me a set of car keys with a flourish. "Is this going to be your first automobile, Mr Harris?"

I admitted that it was.

"Fine. It's the black Dodge in the parking lot next door. It's full of gas and stocked with enough supplies to keep going for three days. Good luck, Mr Harris"

I thanked him, and felt a flicker of excitement at the thought of the Dodge, though Donohue had hinted that the car was on the vintage side. I carried a briefcase holding maps, papers, locations and sites of existing coffee vending machines, and instructions for priming them to drop a plastic cup under a nozzle which would then drop hot water on a teaspoonful of coffee powder.

Pressing another button sent a measure of dried powdered cream to join the coffee at the bottom of the plastic cup. The designer hadn't yet refined the automatic sugar blender to the point of actually working properly, so it was presented separately in a bowl on a table alongside the vending machine. Donohue told me not to be too generous with it, although there was a built-in charge for it in the price of the coffee, whether people took sugar or not.

Half buried under the snow, the Dodge wasn't quite what I expected, and the heavy white flakes connived with Donohue at concealing just how old the car was. I guessed it had first made its way along the production line several years before the Second War— in fact it turned out to be a 1938 model, with a floor starter which had a deafening, long-lasting mechanical stutter which went on sometimes for several minutes before the engine fired. It would never have qualified as a getaway car.

I lifted the lid of what I was learning to refer to as the trunk. There were several bags of coffee and industrial sized cans of dried cream, and a kilo of sugar.

I unlocked the car and tried to slide on to the driver's seat whilst brushing snow off my overcoat. There was a brief crackling sound from the starter, which short-circuited as soon as a flake of snow touched it. I got out of the vehicle, wiped the starter with a handkerchief, and carefully sat down again. This time the starter emitted a stuttering clamour, the engine fired, and the car vibrated

24

expectantly. Carefully, I reversed out of the car park on to the slush of the main road.

The Donohue Harris Coffee Company, or DHC for short, was in business.

CHAPTER FIVE

I left Ennis's and moved into a small flat in a big house in the charming Rosedale district of Toronto, a few streets of gracious buildings regarding each other across the rim of a valley.

My Rosedale residence at 86 Glen Road might once have looked gracious, but its aesthetic quality was somewhat impaired by a moose-head, which had been stuck on the front wall as if the poor beast had charged through the house from the back and got permanently stuck.

My new landlord, Russ Jolley, was the complete opposite of Ennis Rose; he drank a case of lager a day, twelve bottles to a case, and enjoyed occasionally inviting a tenant to dinner, when his long-time lover took an off-night. Russ always referred to her formally as Mrs Rogers.

"Lookut, Walt, Mrs Rogers is eighty-five and I'm sixty, and it bends in the middle," was one of his constant refrains. "Wouldn't likely matter if a beautiful young girl came and sat on my lap, it'd bend in the middle just the same."

After Ennis, Russ was refreshingly secular. His forehead was dominated by a huge wen, and he had evidently made a lifelong investment in the protuberant trelliswork of violet veins which ornamented his face. He was kind and in some ways solitary, like an animal that has known glory in maturity before being eventually cast out of its pack when too old to fight any more for authority.

I couldn't help feeling that his head would one day wind up alongside the moose's.

There was a stables at the back on the far side of the extensive, ragged, largely flower-free garden, and these had been converted into two sizable apartments, holding a dozen young tenants, one for girls and the other for young men. These were for the most part university undergraduates, cheerful and optimistic and heavily engaged biologically and in one or two cases emotionally as well.

Russ liked to think of himself as a marriage broker, and occasionally gave parties for 'his' girls and boys, cooking gigantic steaks to go with the beer. He held one for a number of us on my first evening, and it took as much will-power as I could generate the next morning to exchange the company of the warm and attractive redhead I had wound up spending the night with for that of several dozen highly discontented office workers who had been denied their morning coffee for several weeks. I hoped the coffee machines had at least been cleaned, but it turned out they hadn't been touched.

It was nine o'clock when I arrived at my first port of call, a small advertising agency, as it happened, on a main road called Bloor. Toronto seemed to go in for names devoid of euphony; its biggest supermarket at the time was called Loblaw.

The receptionist was gently flirting with a blonde, fox-faced man wearing a buttoned-down shirt and a suit with a purple and orange check that was a sartorial crime against humanity. "Good morning," the receptionist greeted me. "Do you have an appointment?"

"I've come to see to the coffee machine," I told her. Her welcoming smile turned in a flash into a scowl. "You're the coffee machine man?"

"Well, I'm a partner in the company that's just bought it," I said, conscious that I was wearing the sort of feeble smile that Mickey Mouse was so good at.

"You *bought* it," the man said, cosseting his rage for the benefit of the receptionist, "you don't mean to say you *bought* it, for Chrissake! The fucking coffee tasted as if it was made with dog-shit and arsenic!"

"Well it'll taste much better now that we've taken over," I said, hoping it would. I had my doubts.

"If you think you're going to have any takers for that poison, you've another think coming!" the man snarled. He gave another sideways glance at the receptionist, to make sure that he was amusing her. "Just take the fucking vending machine and get it out of here! We've disconnected it—all you have to do is pick it up and heave it out of the window!"

"It might land on your car," I said.

He bunched his fists. "He's right, Harold," the receptionist intervened, "you usually take the parking space under the window."

"Yeah, well, just get rid of it." Obviously Harold and any coffee I could offer him were irreconcilable.

The vending machine was standing in a defensive attitude with its back to the wall. It looked a bit like a juke box, but instead of a turntable contained a shallow glass dish. In this was floating a green, lumpy liquid that resembled something thrown up by the Sargasso Sea. Nothing would have induced me to drink it myself.

With some difficulty I managed to extract the glass dish; an audience had built up. Nobody showed me much sympathy, and the continuing contagion of Harold's presence didn't help. I put the dish and its contents on a desk.

"Just throw the bile down the toilet!" a man with a green matching tie commanded. He sniggered: "We'll make sure nothing happens to your machine while you're gone."

Resisting the temptation to throw the turgid mixture over him, I did as he had suggested. I had no idea how I was going to dispose of the vending machine without help—maybe it would have to be through the window after all.

When I returned to the office with the empty dish, a tall man with grey hair and pince nez seemed to have restored order. He beckoned me to follow him and led me to a spacious private office.

"I'm sorry they gave you a hard time," he said, "I guess it's a question of punishing someone for sinning without caring if it's the guilty sinner or not. How do you propose to remove your property? Have you got a strong man on the team?"

"We haven't even got a team," I answered.

"All right, I'll ask our janitor and a security guard to carry it out. You'll have to compensate them and provide a removal truck."

"How far is the town dump from here?"

He laughed. "That's probably the right place."

"My partner bought them without realising how long they'd been *in situ* without being serviced."

"Well what you've got in there could never really be described as coffee anyway, I guess." He looked at me pityingly. "Maybe there aren't many worse machines than yours, but there are certainly a lot many better ones. If I may give you some advice, have a look at the market, get yourselves a few new, good quality vending machines so as to be able to compare them, and make sure you know how to service them and do it regularly. If you have to make a choice, always go for quality rather than quantity."

"Thank you. I really appreciate your advice." He took a small metal-bound notebook from his desk and scribbled something. "That's the name of a friend of mine who's got a doughnut factory on the Golden Mile. Stuart Brand's his name. I believe he's looking for a pair of vending machines."

"I'm really grateful for your help."

"Well you sure give the impression you could use some. Now go and rent yourself a truck and I'll have a word with our security people about conveying your property down into the street."

29

I thanked him again. My broadcasting ambitions seemed to be fading beyond distant horizons; perhaps my destiny lay in the world of coffee vending instead, but it wasn't a thought I found in the least consoling.

Donohue had not been pleased by the fact that he had been made to look foolish by buying machines he should have scrapped. I told him that the best thing we could do was to start again, and that if I could persuade Stuart Brand to accommodate our new machines at his doughnut factory on the Golden Mile, we might concentrate on that area and on bakeries, cookie factories and other businesses which cups of drinkable coffee might complement.

There was nothing else for Donohue to do but agree, and a week later two of the latest vending machines on the market had arrived at Stuart's Doughnuts, so that Brand could approve them officially—I had been to the vending machine factory with Donohue to inspect them the previous day.

They seemed to be a considerable improvement over the old ones, and he wrote out a substantial cheque for them. I suspected he was wondering how long it would take to recover his outlay, after I had emptied the machines of cash each day so that I could eat. I suspected also that Russ wouldn't take kindly to receiving his monthly rent of C$100 (Canadian dollars) in metal money, amounting to four hundred coins if paid in quarters, and a thousand if my customers only paid in dimes. The idea of handing Russ the rent and accidentally dropping a thousand coins in small change was scarcely bearable, especially as his living room was full of heavy old furniture for them to hide under.

The Golden Mile was a typical North American strip development that went on for ever, composed of garages, used car lots, fast food joints, factories and showrooms, all stitched together to make a homogenous whole by writhing, restless, neon advertisements flickering in endless arabesques.

I had found it easy to get along with Brand, a big, red-faced man with a bleak beard that seemed to be constructed of fennel. He had a congenial personality and was enthusiastic about the new vending machines—his employees hadn't liked the coffee from the old ones and spent a lot of time visiting various eateries scattered along the Mile, which wasted valuable time. He knew a bar not too far away where the food was eatable and where you could get French wine; he hoped I wouldn't mind driving but his own car was in a garage nearby having new tyres fitted and wouldn't be ready till after lunch.

I told him I'd be happy to drive him, and tried to ignore the expression of disbelief on his face when he saw the Dodge. "It's ideal for ferrying vending machine supplies about," I said with ardent if entirely misplaced loyalty. I lifted the lid of the trunk like a jeweller demonstrating a diamond coronet.

"Yeah," he agreed, "you sure don't want a new Cadillac to transport that stuff."

I trod on the floor starter, which grated loudly. The engine turned and the Dodge began to vibrate. Stuart gave me a few directions as we began to climb the only hill in view and the engine back-fired an expletive. Quickly, the car began to fill with smoke, and Stuart and I hastily thrust our heads out of opposite windows. It wasn't a time for conversation, as the wires began to melt and an acrid and toxic smell began reaching into our lungs. A smoke screen composed of burning rubber, sugar that had begun to caramelise, and scorched milk powder added to the mix. The Dodge shuddered to a stop in surrender.

This was no time for dignity; we flung open our already almost incandescent doors, galloped towards a brick wall and hurled ourselves behind it just as the Dodge exploded. All that was left was a flickering smear on the roadway. Much the same could have been said about my remaining ambitions in the vending machine business.

Stuart and I went our separate ways, and I telephoned Donohue to tell him that I was regretfully resigning our partnership. I felt huge relief at having left him in the lurch.

It was ten o'clock that evening when my phone rang. It was Harry Boyle, to tell me he had finally been reinstated and was now Chairman of CBC Ontario. Would I meet him for a working breakfast tomorrow morning at the King Edward Hotel, which Torontonians called affectionately the King Eddie?

It was a time to take good news for granted, I thought, and raise a glass. As I had nobody to raise one with me, I decided to share the bottle of rye in the drinks cupboard with Russ. Unfortunately my timing wasn't good, as he loudly started to relieve his bladder as soon as I reached the bottom of the back stairs, leaving me trapped between two sets of swing doors which had once opened into the garden from what had been the kitchen. The old serving hatch had been replaced by a sheet of balsa wood over which was tacked a square of wallpaper; I didn't want Russ to know that I was listening to what was an abnormally long performance—it must have been five minutes before I could leave no man's land through the second swing door and quietly slip through on to the landing beyond.

"Now lookut Walt, I'm expecting Mrs Rogers at any minute," he said, peering round the edge of his front door in answer to my knock. He caught sight of the bottle I was carrying. "But as it's you, Son, I guess we've got time for a drop of that Seagram's."

An hour later I gave him the few drops of rye that were left, and returned upstairs. Mrs Rogers hadn't arrived, and Russ had fallen asleep in his armchair.

CHAPTER SIX

Although Harry Boyle was a big man, he seemed to have become bigger than when I had last seen him. Authority was doing him good, pulling his shoulders back and giving his eyes a shrewd sparkle.

There was a bottle of Krug in an ice bucket beside the table, and half a glass of gently fizzing champagne in Harry's fist. He transferred the glass from his right hand to his left to shake hands, and an observant waiter with an eye for a thirsty customer hurried up and poured champagne into my eagerly tilted glass.

"Here's to loyalty," said Harry, as we clicked glasses, "sometimes it's hard to find."

I looked at him. The sparkle in his eyes had turned to a glint. "I take it from what you've just said that someone stabbed you in the back."

"You don't have to be a Caesar to find a Brutus, Walter, and it wasn't a dagger but a letter. Someone who'd expected promotion, didn't get it, and decided I was to blame. She was senior enough to cause me grief. CBC's a pretty political institution and if you're close to the right people you can cause someone quite a lot of grief. Anyhow, I'm back in business now and I'm the person to be close to." He looked like a man who has satisfactorily avenged himself, or was about to.

"I've got a lot to do, and I know you're pretty impatient to get going, so I'm going to accredit you to CBC as a radio journalist, specialising in celebrity interviews. You'll keep your independence but you won't get a salary. You'll get a fee for each interview we broadcast, and you can choose your interviewees, although your producer will have the right to turn down anyone we think unsuitable. Occasionally, we'll give you a feed to someone we particularly want to have on the show, so I'd like you to begin with Ed Sullivan. That'll give your career a good start." He grinned. "If you're going to drop a name, make sure it's a big one. Especially if you're just starting out.

"The programme you'll be principally contributing to is called *Assignment* and it's a flagship programme going out coast to coast, and we want you to interview Ed about two Canadian comics called Wayne and Shuster, who're scheduled to appear on *The Ed Sullivan Show* in three weeks' time."

"Where shall I interview him?"

"He has two apartments, one for business and the other domestic, in the Hotel Delmonico in New York. I expect he'll invite you to come to his office. Wayne and Shuster have been around for some time—in fact they entertained Canadian troops in Europe from about 1944. And they went to Korea during the Korean War and did the same thing there. Have you come across them?"

I admitted I had not even heard of them.

"They're not well known outside Canada yet, but CBC has a very high opinion of them. They tend to go in for literary humour and use Shakespeare and historical figures such as Caesar for their sketches. In fact, one sketch they're doing on the Ed Sullivan show is called *Wash The Blood Off My Toga*. I've watched them do it and they're good.

"I think too it would be a good idea for you to give yourself a few days in New York before you see Sullivan—get yourself acclimatised.

"And make sure you've everything ready before you see him so that you'll be in a reasonably relaxed state. As you've been specially commissioned to do this particular interview, you may claim all expenses and if it's good as I expect you get a bonus. Our usual base

34

rate per interview is in American dollars which as you probably know have an exchange rate value just a little above the Canadian dollar. Incidentally, in future you'll probably find it cheaper to live in Manhattan than to commute from here. The new Vickers Viscount prop-jets are coming into service next month on the Toronto—New York route and that'll cut the journey time to half what it is now. " He smiled.

"Now if you give me your Rosedale address I'll send you the details you need about our New York Office and your accreditation papers."

"Thank you very much, Harry." The fee Harry was offering me was fair, and of course had the great advantage in not being paid in coins.

We each had a five-egg omelette, and finished breakfast with a tumbler of Jack Daniels, the sort of breakfast that was the specialty of a New Orleans restaurant called Brennan's.

"One of the most important things in life is to be able to drink anyone else under the table without showing any effect," Harry said. "Sobriety, even if it's not entirely genuine, can be a damn good weapon." The glint had returned to his eyes again, and I knew the person who had played Brutus was going to be in for a very hard time.

CHAPTER SEVEN

I decided to keep my tiny flat at Russ's and find a modest apartment in the Greenwich Village area of Manhattan. Leaving Russ altogether would mean losing my independence, which I was not prepared to do.

When my CBC accreditation arrived, I took Harry's advice and flew by Viscount to New York. The flight was an entirely new sensation, as the journey, over a distance roughly that between London and Edinburgh, took about fifty minutes, instead of the noisy, laborious couple of hours of the obsolescent aircraft the prop-jet had replaced. The Viscount too had much bigger windows than any other airliner, and they were oval and free of vibration, like the rest of the aeroplane, allowing its passengers to arrive fresh.

I booked in at a Statler which was full, except for a room overlooking an air shaft. In the middle of the night a powerful burst of carbon monoxide turned into a noxious cloud and crept up the shaft into my room; I had the feeling of being strangled in my sleep, which fortunately woke me up. Choking gave way to a headache and a feeling of nausea and I was moved into a staff bedroom. My bill was cancelled.

The next day I started apartment-hunting in the Village and found one on West 8th Street. This was tolerably accessible to Broadway and the Village shops and bars, some of which were devoted to lively little lesbians who all had boys' names and danced vigorously to the music of Bill Haley and Elvis Presley, played on a juke box adjusted to a merciful volume.

By and large the girls were attractive and friendly. One evening I asked a girl called Philip why she only danced with girls and would she give a man a chance? She answered quite seriously: "Honey, you have no idea of the pleasure of holding a woman's body close to yours."

Adding to the unique atmosphere of the area was a Hogarthian women's prison on Lower Sixth Avenue, whose inhabitants often shouted raucous greetings to male passers by and made merrily obscene gestures through the bars.

Toronto was a huge city laterally, which meant it offered its citizens no high compression. New York, on the other hand, and particularly the island of Manhattan, put its citizens under the sort of pressure familiar to laboratory rats.

One chain of cafes, called Choc Full O' Nuts, didn't even offer seating; the customers simply hurried in, carried their purchase to a table, and stood gobbling down their food and swilling a beverage before almost running to re-enter the world outside.

If Manhattan was a peptic ulcer factory, it was also an exciting urban vortex, a place where one didn't think one was missing anything except a civilised life style. It emphasised Rio's glorious indolence and London's doleful shabbiness, it was a city designed for the strangling of tranquillity at birth, except within the fastness of Washington Square where people—usually old men—added scrabble to the historical challenge of chess. Parts of the Square occasionally gave way to demonstrations and protests, emphasising the City's bubbling mixture of paradise and purgatory. New York offered you everything, and if you weren't careful it took everything, it was a pickpocket wearing sables.

On the morning of my appointment with Ed Sullivan, I took a yellow cab from The Village up Fifth towards the Upper East Side. Every traffic light at every block was programmed to change simultaneously, so that there seemed to be an audible click in the split second between red and green.

37

Sharing the back of the taxi with me was the Ampex, reminding me of my unfortunate visit to Brothers Road to interview Ezra Pound. There didn't seem to be an engineer at CBC's Manhattan premises to give me an in-depth tutorial on its use, and the last thing I wanted to do was call Harry for help. I just hoped I knew the machine well enough to record our session successfully.

The Ampex and I arrived at the hotel, and I paid off the cab and asked the cabbie for a receipt as a thin middle-aged flunkie dressed like a bird of Paradise hurried out of the hotel and painfully hefted the Ampex to stagger back across the pavement with it.

"You here to talk to someone famous?" The driver was chewing gum and determined not to look impressed, whatever I answered. "Ed Sullivan," I told him casually.

He whistled, forgetting the gum, which flew out of his mouth and stuck to the windscreen. "That so? Well, famous is the word (he pronounced it 'woid') for Sullivan, I guess."

"I'm looking forward to it," I said cheerfully. How right Harry had been about dropping names that were big.

"Is this for radio?" the driver asked.

"Yes."

"When's it going out?"

"I've no idea." I thanked him for the ride before he could continue grilling me about which broadcasting company I worked for, what sort of fee I was getting and so forth.

"Well, good luck, buddy."

"Thank you. I need it." He drove off and I exchanged the fervour of Park Avenue for the gentle luxury of the Delmonico's lobby. It had, I thought, the atmosphere of a boudoir, a place which at any moment might admit Scheherazade or the Queen of Sheba, pausing to give one a chance to savour their exoticism.

38

I hoisted an Ampex case in each hand and managed to get into an elevator without being caught in the doors.

Ed Sullivan was waiting for me, a man of great dignity with a lugubrious smile and a finely-cut suit perfectly fitting across gorilla-like shoulders.

I apologised for being late, although I wasn't, and he took the part of the Ampex containing the recording deck and put it on a side table. "I'd say you were absolutely on time." He smiled. "Now I believe you want to talk with me about the two Canadian comics who are appearing on my show."

"That's right, Mr. Sullivan."

"Ed will do, Walter. Or is it Walt?"

"Walter, please."

"Fine." I had done my best to prime the Ampex before my arrival, to avoid unnecessary delay; the spools were in place and hopefully I had laced them up properly.

I smiled at Ed, pressed the start button, and asked the first question. Was he familiar with the work of Wayne and Shuster?

He'd seen recordings of some of their shows, and thought they were good.

Was there much difference between Canadian and American humour?

There were certain general differences—Canadian humour tended to be more literate but American wit was sharper on the whole. Wayne & Shuster's act went in for classical allusions, as Harry had briefed me, and based some of their work on historical and literary events. In fact, Wayne & Shuster were eventually to appear more than anyone else on the *Ed Sullivan Show*, some sixty to seventy times in just over a decade.

After ten minutes or so, the interview ended and it was playback time. I switched the tape to fast rewind and held my breath as it moved on to play mode.

The recording was a disaster. The background noise was so loud there was nothing background about it, it was a foreground static roar which levelled every cadence and siphoned out all meaning.

Ed smiled and patted my shoulder. "That's the trouble with Manhattan, Walter. There's always so much traffic noise. Comes out on the recording tape like the sound of a hurricane. Do you mind if I try a little adjustment?"

"I'm very sorry, Ed."

"Don't worry, it happens all the time. Maybe I'll go and live somewhere quiet one day. Right, let's do it again."

It was a longer interview and it was unblemished. Harry Boyle would probably have given me another chance anyway, but I would have been mortified at having made a fool of myself.

As it was, Ed Sullivan had helped to enhance my chances of a successful career.

A week after the interview, I found myself at a film première, with a large crowd beginning already to build up outside the theatre. I lugged the Ampex into the foyer, waved my press card, and put the twin cases on a long shelf, much of which was already covered by tape recorders presided over by reporters.

The system was that the first reporter would corral the first star to enter the foyer, ask one or two fairly fatuous questions, and then go into a sort of fire pail routine, taking the star by the elbow and handing whoever it was over to the next reporter in line. The process was repeated, either till the star had had enough and stood panting and dishevelled at the far end of the row, or simply fought back, which could incur the wrath of publicity-hunting studio bosses back in Hollywood.

To my dismay, I found that the elbow I had seized was that of Ginger Rogers, who wasn't even in the movie featured at the première, whose star was in fact the Mexican comedian, Fernandel. I was even more appalled to hear myself addressing her as 'Ginge', like the reporter who had handed her over to me. I hate to think what puerile question or comment I shouted at her.

The next metaphorical pail to swing into my clutches was Bob Hope, who was also not in the movie. Christian Dior had created a new style of *haute couture* which was shapeless and naturally very expensive. It was called the sack dress and so, having read in a movie magazine that Bob Hope had been travelling in Russia, I asked him if he had come across any sack dresses there.

"Not sack dresses," Hope said, "but I visited Moscow, and there they go in for sack bodies." I knew he was alleged to have a quip—or at least a writer—for every occasion, but it seemed fair to give him the benefit of the doubt as to whether or not his wit was impromptu, as he had no idea I was going to mention sack dresses. Neither did I.

A Broadway friend of mine was an English actress called Myra Carter, who introduced me to a number of her friends and colleagues. One was the actress, Siobhán MacKenna, whom we went to meet in her cabin on the Cunarder *Caronia* on her arrival from Liverpool.

Siobhán, who had learnt her craft at Dublin's Abbey Theatre, had a soft Irish voice expressing a passionate nature which made her performances supremely memorable. She had come over to star opposite a well-known actor of the day, Art Carney, in Enid Bagnold's play *The Chalk Garden*. Eli Wallach was also a protagonist, and so was an actress with strangely luminous eyes I had been attracted to in my teens, Joan Blondell. After that, Siobhán and Art Carney starred in another Broadway play, *The Rope Dancers*.

Siobhán had the sort of wild Irish beauty which so vividly made its mark on her nation. Her husband, Denis O'Dea, was a fine

41

thespian too, but I never met him. Siobhán's voice is still with me, and not only because I recorded it.

I can hear her, and in my mind's eye see her, as she stood downstage centre, her voice resounding in every part of the theatre; she used emotional language in a way that made it impossible not to weep, the passion pouring out of her, her long dark hair a moving frame for her beautiful, expressive face.

She had a generous thirst and a heart to match, but over-estimated the robustness of her genes. She was still quite young when the whisky got her, and died of cancer at the age of sixty-three.

Gertrude Lawrence was another actress who died young, and one of the most poignant stories I came across on Broadway concerned her.

A Broadway stage-door keeper I knew called Snap Henderson greeted me one afternoon as a Phantom Five Rolls Royce limousine drew up. A kindly-looking, hippo-shaped black man climbed out from behind the wheel.

"Now that's somebody you ought to meet," Snap said, after the two had exchanged greetings and the driver had gone inside. "He's probably got more stories he could tell you about Broadway than anyone else in town. His name's Roosevelt Zanders. You see that Rolls Royce car? That's the flagship of his fleet of limousines. Just bought it, after running the business for years. Started with a Buick Roadmaster.

"You're a big star and you don't want to hang around for a cab after rehearsal? Roosevelt'll run you home. You want to be picked up at home and brought to the theatre every night? Take a Zanders chauffeur-driven hire. He's dedicated, Roosevelt. And all his drivers give the same sort of service.

"Before long he buys another Roadmaster, and then a Caddie. Then he gets the idea of buying a classic limo especially for society weddings. What does he get for them? First a Duesenberg and then a 1913 Pierce Arrow. Set him back about eight hundred thousand bucks at the Black Hawk auto auction at Pebble Beach." He looked round to indicate that he was about to tell me something confidential and didn't want witnesses.

"You ask Roosevelt about driving Gertrude Lawrence. That's a story, but he doesn't really like talking about it."

Zanders came back through the stage door before I could ask Snap why I should broach a subject Zanders didn't like discussing. "Hey, Roosevelt, this fellow's from England. Broadcaster for Canadian radio. You talk to him. Guess he'd like to interview you."

Roosevelt and I shook hands. "Interviewing is O.K. but I don't do gossip," he said. "The people who hire my cars are my friends, and they trust me not to gossip about them."

"I'm not interested in gossip. But from what Snap said you know a lot of Broadway people. Maybe you could tell me a story about a person or experience that stands out in your mind, a human interest story." He scrutinised my face to assess my trustworthiness.

"Well, I guess I can do that. Shall we drive around Central Park? I somehow concentrate better behind the wheel."

I looked at the huge maroon Rolls with its scrupulously clean white sidewall tyres. "Central Park would be fine."

"Good." He picked up the Ampex and put the beige leather cases on the back seat.

"Do you mind if I sit in front, Roosevelt—or do I call you Mr. Zanders?"

"Roosevelt's fine. And your name?"

I introduced myself. "Snap's a bit impulsive sometimes," Roosevelt said. "But he's a good friend. Good PR man, too." Snap grinned at him. I reached round to pick up the microphone and switch on the recorder, and Roosevelt took the slender steering-

43

wheel and slid his fingers in their black leather gloves into the wheel's sculpted finger-holds. Snap went back through the stage door. I mentioned Gertrude Lawrence.

"She was one of my favourite people," Zanders said, as we set off. "She and Noël Coward had been at the same school of acting and became lifelong friends. I'd met her once or twice with him when he came here to watch her rehearse. He had a play on Broadway— Present Laughter, I think it was called. I forget who took over the lead from Mr. Coward –actor called Hugh Sinclair, I believe. Mr. Coward didn't like to spend too much time in one of his stage plays—six months was about the most he would do. Got bored after that, but I guess he was the only person who did."

A yellow cab went by and the city resounded with the shrill warnings of klaxons and the undulating scream of sirens. Bedraggled birds tried to balance comfortably on the branches of leafless trees.

"Did you drive Gertrude Lawrence when she was playing opposite Yul Brynner in *The King and I,* Roosevelt?"

He stared straight ahead, looking sad and to some degree defensive. "That's right."

"Would you mind telling me about it?"

He turned his large head to glance at me briefly. "This is for a broadcast, right?"

"Yes, for The Canadian Broadcasting Corporation. A flagship programme called *Assignment*, which is transmitted coast to coast."

He nodded. "There are some people I don't respect enough to discuss Miss Lawrence with them." He sighed.

"She liked me to drive her; we got on well together. I knew when she wanted to talk and when she just wanted to relax. She was well into rehearsals for The King and I some time in late 1950 or early January '51 when she began to feel bad. As the show premiered, I recall, on March 29th 1951 I guess it was January when she really started hurting.

"She went to Mount Sinai Hospital but even there nobody seemed to be able to diagnose exactly what was wrong with her. I rearranged my schedule and became her chauffeur exclusively, picking her up at home and taking her to the theatre and waiting to run her back each evening after the show.

"One evening she asked me not to run her home straight away. She wanted time to unwind, but she always hid the pain so well nobody knew about it. She laughed a lot too, though she could get mighty mad if something really upset her. But that first evening she asked me to run her round Central Park while she did her best to heal herself. She was quiet, just lay back on the squab of the back seat after opening the partition and didn't say a word. I heard her cry out once or twice, and I wanted to stop and see if there was anything I could do, but I knew that wasn't what she wanted.

"So I just drove, making the ride as smooth as I could, and after a while I thought she really was asleep, so I took her home and helped her up the steps. Someone came out and we supported her so she could get inside the house.

"After that it became a sort of habit to drive Miss Lawrence round Central Park, give her a chance to let go. As the pain got worse she asked me to keep as far away from other traffic as I could, so there was less chance of anyone hearing her cry out, though they wouldn't have seen or heard much as she was lying below the window line.

"But next day, no matter how sick she felt, she'd give a brilliant performance, taking over the stage with that personality of hers even if Mr. Brynner was standing on stage right alongside her.

"It was later on, in the back of my car, that she acted even better. Even I thought sometimes that the pain had gone, but of course it hadn't."

"Did they find out what was the matter with her?" I asked.

"I think she died before they found out it was liver cancer. It was a very private dying."

"Did it happen when she was in your car?"

"She died a little each day, like the song says. Nothing I could do about it. You know, it's not only people in the military should get medals for bravery. Theatre folk say "the show must go on" and other people think that's quite comical, maybe because theatre people are so self-conscious about everything they do.

"But Miss Lawrence, she was something special, she was Gertrude Lawrence the Lionheart, she was set on fighting to a standstill. She lay along the back seat of my car and cursed the Lord for the pain she was in." He sighed. "Because the show that had to go on was her life." He stopped the Rolls just beyond the horses and carriages waiting for custom outside the Plaza, and I thanked him as he got out with the Ampex cases and handed them to a porter.

"I'm not staying here," I told him, "I just fancy a drink." The porter arranged custody for the cases in the cloakroom and I shook hands with Roosevelt and made my way to a bar.

Even on a soggy winter's afternoon you could feel the ardent throb of the city's pulse; but only a week previously I had seen a dead man, a candle burning at each side of his head, lying on the pavement of 42nd.Street, a block or two from Times Square. Nobody had time to stop, but a parked Oldsmobile moved to make space for the hearse.

I sat on a bar stool; there seemed only one simple and immediate antidote to nature's darker caprices, so I ordered a large dry martini.

46

CHAPTER EIGHT

I flew back to Toronto just before Christmas. Russ Jolley's house was in apparent mourning, a sign that the festive season had arrived. Russ hated Christmas with his own unique brand of misanthropy; he loathed gaiety and false spontaneity, as he saw it, and at the first hint of a carol took to his rooms like a mouse to its hole.

His greatest fear, as it turned out, was that his son might try to visit him with his family. Russ was appalled at the idea of having a family which might impose itself on his privacy over Christmas. When I arrived at the house, he greeted me with what I can best describe as sour warmth, peering anxiously behind me as I advanced to shake his hand, in case the family might be using my shoulders as a shield behind which to hide. Reassured they weren't, he gave me a partial hug and let me inside.

I was spending a couple of days in my flat and Christmas Eve and Christmas Day at Port Credit with George and Alison Hellman. After a meeting with Harry Boyle I was flying back to New York for New Year's Eve with a girl friend called Grania.

The day before Christmas Eve a Molson Brewery truck arrived in Russ's rather shabby driveway with springs fully compressed under its load, to be expertly emptied by two men over a period of a half hour or so—Russ was not of course celebrating Christmas, just making sure he wouldn't have to endure a drought if he ran out of booze before the New Year.

As soon as the Saviour's birthday was safely in the past, he told me, he was launching a New Year's Eve Party 'for my boys and girls', and as midnight struck would lead Mrs. Rogers on the path to glory under the mistletoe.

"Lookut Walt, if things go right who knows, it mightn't bend in the middle for once," he said in a rare moment of optimism after his third beer. The wen on his forehead seemed to crackle a cheerful endorsement. "If she can forget I'm getting on for seventy, I should be able to forget she's accelerating towards eighty."

I arrived back at Kennedy—which with the future President's assassination six years away was still called Idlewild—on the snow-laden morning of New Year's Eve 1956. My visit to Toronto had been blurred but enjoyable, and my brain had recorded it montage style, with Russ's and Mrs. Rogers's faces spinning round intermingled with George's and Alison Hellman's, whilst Harry Boyle grinned at me over his shoulder.

Grania was an air hostess with Aer Lingus, and shared an apartment at Queen's with several girls working for other airlines. When I came to pick her up she had only been home for a short time, having been delayed by bad weather. The average journey time between Dublin and New York in those days was approximately twelve hours, but Grania looked as fresh as though she had just begun the flight. We had a drink and took a taxi to Manhattan, where I had booked a table at a night club called The Blue Angel.

The evening was memorable. I had heard of nobody on the bill, which was headed by a couple called Elaine May and Mike Nichols, whose cabaret act was sophisticated and immensely stylish. They shone as if polished, and were long legged in the Californian way, although Nichols had been born in Germany. May was to become over the ensuing years a very well-known song-writer and entertainer, whilst Nichols evolved into a highly successful stage and screen director whose credits were to include *The Undergraduate; Who's Afraid of Virginia Woolf?* and *Catch 22,* and whom Elizabeth Taylor more than once demanded as her director.

Immediately below May and Nichols on the billing came Tom Lehrer, a young Harvard Professor of Mathematics.

He had a uniquely plangent voice and a gift for making even his piano sound sardonic. The phrase usually applied to him when he became well-known was that he was 'an acquired taste', in which case his cult lost little time in acquiring it. He shared Danny Kaye's ability to speed-sing and handle complex lyrics with uncluttered elegance, wit and timing, but unlike Kaye leavened his lyrics with doses of humorous cruelty.

Lehrer rejoiced in profaning the sacred, sending up the Roman Catholic liturgy: in *Vatican Rag*, for example, where he called the congregation to "Genuflect! Genuflect! Genuflect!"

When discussing famous people from history Lehrer referred with delicately crafted scorn to Franz Werfel as the 'author of The Song of Bernadette and other masterpieces', adding that: "It's people like that who make you realise how little you've accomplished. It's a sobering thought, for example, that when Mozart was my age he'd been dead for two years."

One of the more poignant interviews I carried out in New York was with a Russian Jewish impresario called Sol Hurok.

Like so many people of Russian origin whose families emigrated from the sorrows and dangers of Tsarist Russia—most of the founders of Hollywood; the Gershwins; the Berlins—Hurok arrived to live permanently in America when he was not yet twenty. When I met him he was approaching sixty, a solidly-built man with a large and impressive bald head and a thick accent that had probably not changed much in forty years.

Hurok's achievements, which changed the musical landscape of the world and particularly of Russia and America, were profound. Whether self-imposed or forced on him by the pogroms committed by sword-wielding Cossacks as they charged on their ponies through the cities and farms of his birthplace in the Ukrainian Delta, the impresario used his lifelong exile in America to bare and display to each other the passionate and artistic souls of Russian ballet and American Dance, as he defined them. Under his auspices the Bolshoi Ballet of Moscow, the Ballet Russe de Monte Carlo and the Kirov of Leningrad made their first appearances in America, and subsequently toured every few years.

Hurok's huge client list—during his career it reached a total of some four thousand artists—included the opera singer Marian Anderson and an elysian coterie of musicians such as David and Igor Oistrakh; Segovia, Sviatoslov Richter and Ashkenazy.

It was evident that love of the arts, not money, gave Hurok the inspired empathy which existed between him and his clients. He spoke of them as his personal friends, and said that if their relationship had been simply professional, he would have chosen to make a career at something else, as being an impresario was principally a matter of friendship and personal contact, rather than just money.

His office walls were a sort of encyclopaedia of the arts, and brought to life people I had read about or knew only from research done prior to meeting Hurok. Early in his career, he had acquired two dancers as clients who were utterly different in their approaches to their art, Pavlova and Isadora Duncan.

Pavlova was born to become a world-famous prima ballerina, even though she suffered from ankles so slender she had to have specially shaped and reinforced dancing shoes, and only because of her genius was able to dispense with certain traditional but ruinously uncomfortable ballet movements which even her carefully crafted footwear could not support.

As a prima ballerina, she was able to bypass having to dance her way through the chorus to solo status, but went straight to the top, as did another Hurok ballet dancer, Margo Fontaine.

Isadora Duncan, on the other hand, called herself a free dancer and often danced barefoot.

She regarded ballet as restrictive and was a feminist and apostle of Dionysius; she believed that her performance should be untrammelled by any sort of choreographic convention.

Her love of freedom did not save her from becoming a Communist, and going to live in the Soviet Union after Hurok had arranged a dancing tour for her there. She married a Russian poet called Sergei Essenine so that he could qualify as an immigrant to the United States, even though he was an alcoholic and constantly beat her.

I never met her; as apart from anything else she died just after I was born. However, I felt a strange intimacy with her, as one day I was handed the instrument of her death at the New York Public Library, where I was researching a magazine article about her soon after my Hurok interview.

An attendant handed me a fragment of red silk, frayed and crumpled. It came from the shawl which Isadora habitually wore onstage when dancing her interpretation of the Marseillaise.

She had been killed by the shawl in 1927 in Nice in a bizarre accident.

According to Mary Desti, a friend who witnessed it, the dancer had been wearing the shawl when she impulsively leaped into a stationary open sports car—allegedly a Bugatti—driven by a handsome young Italian mechanic.

"Je vais à la gloire!" she shouted.

As the car pulled away from the kerb, the shawl billowed out behind Isadora and caught in the spokes of the rear wheel, slamming her head against the side of the car and strangling her as it jerked her into the road. It was in a way a fitting death for a woman whose life had generated so much publicity.

In 1931 Pavlova died, at the age of fifty-four. In its way her death was also bizarre, resulting from pneumonia caused by a railway accident at The Hague. Pavlova was returning from the South of France, where she had been on holiday, to her Dutch home in which she lived with her Belgian husband.

Although not hurt in the accident, she was trapped in light summer clothes for twelve hours afterwards on The Hague's snow-laden station platform, from which she couldn't escape.

When I met Sol Hurok both artists had been dead for nearly a quarter of a century, but in his office, with its photographs and memorabilia of them, they still appeared vividly alive. Emanating from them, however, was an aura of frustration at lives cut short, an expression of posthumous resentment in their sepia-tinted eyes.

Hurok was to live until the age of eighty-five, dying of a heart attack on his way to arrange with David Rockefeller the plans and finance for a special appearance on the American stage of Rudolf Nureyev.

CHAPTER NINE

In 1925 The New Yorker Magazine was born under the editorship of Harold Ross in the bar of Manhattan's Algonquin Hotel at 59 West Forty-Fourth Street. The group included the writer and humorist Robert Benchley and Dorothy Parker, a poet and cynic with a savage wit and an obsession with suicide and ways of achieving it, but for others rather than herself. It was something of a surprise to her friends—and perhaps a disappointment—that she lived to be seventy-three and died of natural causes. After all, she had written in one of her poems:

> Drink and dance and love and lie,
> Love, the reeling midnight through,
> For tomorrow we shall die!
> (But, alas, we never do.)

In 1935 The New Yorker took on a young artist whose cartoons were humorous but had a strong leaning towards the macabre. Charles Addams was born in New Jersey and trained to be an architect, thus learning a draftsman's precision. I had heard that every so often he underwent periods of insanity which induced the magazine to send him to recuperate in a mental hospital.

In his office at the New Yorker, which he invited me to visit after I had telephoned to ask him for an interview, there was an unpublished etching pinned to the wall. It portrayed a naked old man peering at a girl through the wrong end of a telescope, and was captioned *The Elderly Pervert*.

Addams himself had crisp short hair, a bulbous nose and humorous eyes; after the interview we went for a drink at the Algonquin Bar and he mentioned that a few nights previously he had dined with Marilyn Munroe and Arthur Miller.

"She had eyes like blue searchlights," Addams told me, "and she and Miller were playing footsie under the table, except it was sometimes my foot she rubbed hers against by mistake. It was hard for me."

Another New Yorker cartoonist, Whitney Darrow, invited me to visit him at his house in Connecticut. During the course of the evening he presented me with a volume of his work, which included an illustration depicting an infuriated husband glaring at his wife as they stand by the french windows after a dinner party, as the last guest disappears through the garden gate.

"When I say stop me if you've heard this one, I don't mean you!" snarls the caption.

My interest in cartoonists and their craft burgeoned when I started to augment my RAF pay of just over £3 a fortnight as an RAF flight mechanic in 1944. I sent several ideas for cartoons and their captions to Kenneth Bird, the Art Editor of Punch, who accepted some for publication. Bird drew under the pen name of *Fougasse*, and during the War became famous for a series of posters for the Ministry of Information about the dangers of public indiscretion. The series was called generically *Careless Talk Costs Lives*.

After several months in New York, I decided it was time to go back to England. I had been away, apart from a three month interval to see my family and visit the Festival of Britain in 1951, for ten years. Harry assured me I would continue to be accredited to CBC, and saw no reason why I should not broadcast the same interviews on the BBC. Broadcasting experience in North America was respected in Britain and regarded as being polished and well performed, if often irritating.

I went up to Toronto for dinner with Harry and a final visit to the Hellmans, who drove me to Malton, Toronto's international airport, the following morning. The long and graceful Britannia prop jet, which had recently gone into service with British Overseas Airways Corporation (BOAC) and cut the journey time across the Atlantic by about half, swept elegantly into the sky and soon began to settle into the rhythm of our long flight.

Strangely, I felt an apprehension at returning to my own country that I hadn't had when leaving it. It was the known that held a threat; the unknown never had. My father was waiting for me at Heathrow; he was a dapper man clad by the retailers of St. James—hats by Locke, shoes by Lobb, ties by Sulka, shirts by Hawes & Curtis, suits by Sullavan & Williams of Savile Row.

Smoking accessories: pipes by Dunhill, cigarettes by Rothman or W.D.& H.O.Wills and Rothman's; cigars by Cuba, usually Partagas or Romeo y Julietta. Our relationship had never been loving, at least on his side, and both he and my mother had divorced and remarried fifteen years previously, in 1943. My stepmother, Eileen, was fourteen years younger than my father, and had modelled stockings before the Second War; my stepfather, Rhys Thomas, had been a fighter pilot in the Battle of Britain, and worn the medal ribbons of the DFC and DSO, only to die of peritonitis after seven years of marriage.

"He must have found something in your mother I missed," was my father's sour post mortem comment.

Now here he was wearing a rakish green trilby tilted across his small bald head, the hat matching the green eyes which welcomed me with a quizzical scrutiny. He sat behind the wheel of a new Humber Hawk with a red leather interior, black sunshine roof and pale grey body. It made the doors of the arrivals building outside which it was parked look even shabbier than they were.

The first view of London offered to the new arrival was not encouraging. The Queen's Building and the control tower were the only ones laying any claim to permanence; the others were Nissen huts like tawdry mushrooms, surrounded by quagmires of wet mud. My father leaned towards me and pushed open the passenger door and I felt a surge of filial affection..

"Hello, Dad." I kissed his cheek, managing to avoid the trilby.

"Welcome home. How was the flight?"

"Very pleasant. Prop jets are so much smoother than piston engines."

"So I understand." The filial affection wavered as formality clung to us adhesively.

With most people I enjoyed communication, and after all made my living from talking to them; my father was inclined to be taciturn with me and once told my stepmother I had no conversation. I knew he felt affronted at my refusal to join him in the family business, furnishing cinemas and town halls, but I wasn't suited to it. Working with my father would have been like becoming a Trappist monk, speaking little and in winter sharing a cell with a small gas fire as trains rumbled hesitantly overhead.

We drove through London's dismaying outskirts almost in silence. The city was like a vast buffet offering only stale food and blight. The broken teeth of ruined buildings bit feebly into a sere landscape, and in many cases all that remained of them had been turned into car parks.

In these, most of the cars surrounded by concrete holes filled with water laced with oil were almost all pre-war models, as new ones were severely rationed in the cause of export. My father had acquired his Humber from a showroom in Cowes, in the Isle of Wight, after a tip-off from a friend in the motor business.

For my first two weeks back in England I spent a few days with my father in London, where he and Eileen lived in a block of flats called Bryanston Court, not far from Broadcasting House in Portland Place and before the War the home of Wallis Simpson and her husband, until the Prince of Wales began to call.

I spent the rest of my time with my mother at her flat in Chelsea. It was much smaller than my father's, in a building called Chesil Court, and overlooked the Thames at Cheyne Walk. Our relationship had always been close but there was the scent of a second stepfather in the air, a pleasant, ponderous man whose legs had been badly shot up on the battlefields of the Somme and whose breathing was impaired by emphysema caused by his inhalation of chlorine gas in the trenches. I liked him but we had little in common.

I felt somehow guilty for what had been inflicted on him by the authorities of his own generation.

Chesil Court was also inhabited by Lord Longford and his dynasty; he often used to stand in the lobby, meditating in front of the lift gates. A gentle and intelligent man and the head of a distinguished literary family, he nearly became a public enemy by his habit of visiting the child murderer Myra Hyndley in gaol and trying to get her a substantial remission of her life sentence.

On the other side of Chesil Court was Swan Court, a much larger block. Among its inhabitants were several aristocrats of the Arts, including an eminent architect, Sir Lewis Casson and his actress wife Dame Sybil Thorndike, who was tall and classically sculpted in word and appearance, a Roedean gel from Dionysian Greece.

A regular diner in Swan Court's public rooms was another Dame, Agatha Christie, who was short and plump and wore her gray hair in a bun. It was difficult to imagine how much cerebral energy her brain cells must have generated over the years; I imagined coils of plots rotating and interweaving under her skull rather than, like the serpents of the Medusa, on top of it.

Yet for one so adept at contriving murder, Agatha Christie seemed remarkably benign, someone for whom even the concept of evil barely existed, yet someone who must have been all too aware of how little profit there is in innocence.

CHAPTER TEN

I managed to find a one-room flat in Forset Court, a block of flats in the Edgware Road. Bryanston Court, my father's block in George Street, was five minutes' walk away, the BBC twenty minutes, and my mother's flat a half hour by bus.

Opposite my flat was a Chinese restaurant, the Lotus House, owned by a suave and charming Chinese called Johnny Koon, whose father had founded the Cathay in Piccadilly Circus, London's first Chinese restaurant. Johnny claimed to have introduced automatic car washes into England, but concentrated on making the Lotus a sort of gastronomic filling station attracting the kind of home-grown and Hollywood gastronomes who cherished the difference between the cuisines of Canton and Peking. He eventually eloped to Tangiers with Gerry, his young head waiter.

Interviewing or associating with people wrapped in highly developed egos usually known as star quality did offer a unique stimulus. The opening of a new stage play or film brought glamour to London, and to those of us trying to find new talent or reintroduce well-known stars there was in London a constant source of supply, and specialist magazines which posted news each week to their subscribers of famous thespians visiting London, the reason for their visit, and where they would be staying.

The two hotels most favoured by showbiz stars were The Savoy and The Dorchester, although The Ritz was the hostelry chosen by the raucous American musical actress Elaine Stritch as her London home during even quite long runs on the West End stage. Claridge's was where aspirant English aristocrats looked for American business heiresses in order to give them transfusions of blue blood in exchange for transfusions of cash to repair tax-ravaged estates.

At the Dorchester public relations was for some twenty-five years in the hands of a capable, near-omniscient woman called Marjorie Lee, through whom I met people as diverse as Somerset Maugham and Hugh O'Bryan, who played Wyatt Earp in the long-running 1950s and 60s Wild West series.

The Connaught was particularly favoured by top flight editors and journalists, including Alistair Cook, and gourmet thespians such as Peter Ustinov, as it was reputed to have the finest hotel chef in London.

So far as I was concerned, the Savoy was the best equipped for the professional seeker after film and stage thespians, having a press room staffed by several attractive girls who dealt out information and Scotch in generous measures.

One morning Marjorie Lee phoned me. Her voice was both warm and crisply efficient. "You've often mentioned Noël Coward in the past as someone you wanted to interview, but could never get hold of. I wasn't encouraging, because interviewers fall into one of the rather large category of people he detests. However, he's staying here till tomorrow on a migration between his house in Jamaica and his Swiss home at Montreux-les-Avants, and he's just published his first novel, Pomp and Circumstance. You never know, he might be interested in getting some publicity for it. Good time to have a go, perhaps." She gave me the number of his suite, wished me good luck and hung up before I could thank her.

Coward answered immediately in the famous light, clipped voice which went up in intonation at the end of a sentence. He was prepared to give me an interview, but evidently not to make things easy for me—he was catching an early flight to Geneva and suggested we meet in the Queen's Building at Heathrow the following morning at five thirty. I acceded.

Coward was perhaps the most accomplished all-round entertainer of the twentieth century; playwright, composer, actor, director, pianist and wit and raconteur. He had dared to stage a play featuring a rich young cocaine-addict—*The Vortex,* when he was only twenty-two—which had had to open at a fringe theatre, the Everyman in Hampstead, because at first West End managements were afraid to stage anything so controversial. Coward's understudy was John Gielgud. His play *Brief Encounter* was the most distinguished tear-jerker of the Second World War.

I parked my car as near the Queen's Building as possible and lugged the tape recorder along a corridor towards our rendezvous point about two hundred yards away. Heathrow had its usual aura of trench warfare in the morning gloom.

Whilst the tape recorder, an EMI, had a bulky wooden frame covered by green imitation leather and wasn't quite as big and heavy as an Ampex, it nevertheless had the shoulder-dislocating bulk and size of a large picnic hamper. The only person in sight was a yawning official in customs uniform, so I paused to have a word with him.

"Could you do something for me, please?"

His yawn at once narrowed into thin-lipped suspicion. "I'm not supposed to do things for people," he said. "I'm with Customs and Immigration."

"Yes, that's why I'd like your assistance. I'm meeting Noël Coward for an interview in a few minutes, and I'd be very grateful if you could see that he gets through the turnstile afterwards without having to wait for ages, as there'll probably be a long queue by then to get into the departure lounge."

61

"Not sure I'd recognise him." Someone came through a distant door and walked towards us. "That him?"

"I've never seen him in the flesh, but in his films and photographs he's always immaculately groomed and clean-shaven."

"I can see that chap's stubble from here," the official commented. "Nothing exactly dapper about his hat, either. All right, I'll see he gets through the mob afterwards without hindrance."

"Thank you," I said, and turned to walk towards the man known among thespians as 'The Master'. He saw with evident satisfaction that I was out of breath and shook hands.

He was unrecognisable as 'Mr. Coward in his dressing-gown exquisitely flowered', as Hermione Gingold sang of him with gentle malice during the War in *Sweet and Low* , a long-running Alan Melville revue in the West End.

Usually suave, beardless as a porcelain platter and as precise in his looks as in his movements, the portrait Coward presented now was the antithesis of his usual appearance. I could almost sense the rising sun flinch as it encountered his sacerdotal, wideawake hat, black coat and face sprinkled with piebald stubble. He looked like a recently unfrocked priest.

Having greeted him and introduced myself I started by asking about his novel.

"I enjoyed it. It's a cheerful book, I hope." We went on to discuss contemporary theatre, which had wrung the neck of traditional theatre with the strong literary wrists of Pinter's The Caretaker and Osborne's Look Back In Anger. What, I asked Coward, did he think of that sort of modernist play usually referred to as The Kitchen Sink School?

"I think very little of that sort of play, as a matter of fact."

I remarked that some of the critics seemed to like them. Were they perhaps intoxicated with their own cleverness?

"I am not aware of much cleverness and of very little sign of intoxication. They tend to be very earnest, and they do have something else in common." He arched his eyebrows and added: "they are almost completely ignorant of the theatre."

I laughed; he was a man with a wonderful capacity for disdain. "I've thought for some time what a pity it is that Edison didn't invent the phonograph a good deal earlier than 1880."

"He did his best," Coward said, and asked me to elaborate.

"Because of all the voices we were destined never to hear. All the actors and actresses, poets and playwrights and so on, whose voices we missed because the phonograph hadn't been invented."

"Perhaps a well-disguised blessing. Think of all the nonsense we've been spared."

"There is that." I decided to take a chance to mention something I had been considering for some time. "We still don't have an archival record on the theatre, Mr. Coward. Would you be willing to contribute to one? My idea is to invite a group of thespians at various stages of their age and significance to participate so that their voices and current views on every aspect of theatre as they perceive them at the time will be on record permanently."

"Very well," Coward said without hesitation, and to my delight mentioned neither his agent nor a fee. "Call me or my secretary Cole Leslie at home at Montreux-les-Avants and make an appointment to come over for luncheon. I'll do the recording afterwards." He gave me his card.

On a high, I escorted him to the turnstiles, which by then were swirling with travellers like lock gates trying to control the displacement of a liner. Good temper was being replaced by rage.

"I've made arrangements for you to go through straight away, Mr. Coward." I said, looking anxiously round for the official I'd spoken to. He was nowhere in sight. I reached out for Coward's languid right hand for a farewell shake.

"Good bye," I said, "Thank you very much." As I turned away an angry voice shouted at The Master: "who the fuck do you think you are, pushing in like that?"

I fled, before Coward could rescind his invitation.

CHAPTER ELEVEN

The next participant I recruited for the theatre project was Peter Ustinov. We met in the BBC's TV studios at Lime Grove, not long after he had won an Academy Award for his performance as the slave broker in *Spartacus*.

Lime Grove would have provided a suitable background for *The Flintstones*; it had somehow managed to acquire a prehistoric atmosphere even though the BBC had only one channel at the time, and only one daytime television programme to appear on it once a week.

This was *Wednesday Magazine*; as its name indicated, it was only screened on Wednesdays. It was—and still is—the function of a TV magazine programme to be a sort of pixel potpourri, a series of events or portrayals of various news items which might possibly be of interest to a common denominator of viewers, and not necessarily one that was the lowest.

The director of *Wednesday Magazine,* Dick Francis, was a young, tough, ruddy-faced Yorkshireman who had joined the BBC a few months previously as an associate radio producer to a producer called John Bridges, who did not appreciate his assistant's having transferred to television as soon as he could.

I liked Dick, but it had to be admitted hat he suffered from a surplus of ambition. Like most highly ambitious people he was immune to the disapproval of others, and had no time for any mobility that wasn't upward. He gave me the impression of being a career gibbon, swinging his prehensile way through the BBC's promotional highways far above those content to remain nearer ground level.

I had dropped by out of curiosity to see him directing the programme one Wednesday, and was fortunate that Peter Ustinov was one of his guests, a warm, burly, Spanish-Main-style figure with a black beard. He had an uncannily mellifluous laugh. The other guest was the author Elizabeth Jane Howard.

Dick offered to drive us back to the centre of London, and Ustinov and I sat in the back of his Sunbeam Rapier, whilst Elizabeth Jane Howard sat next to Dick. She had been married to the great ornithologist and champion of birds, Sir Peter Scott, and later on was to be the wife of Kingsley Amis. She struck me as being majestic, or perhaps simply aloof, but Dick showed signs of being attracted to her, leaning confidentially towards her ear whilst keeping his eyes on the road, or extending his own for a hoped-for confidence.

By the time we dropped Ustinov off at the Connaught, he and I had arranged to meet at the hotel the following week for me to record his views on the theatre for the archival project. It was time for me to find an appropriate record company.

There were only two which were of real interest: one, Caedmon, had been founded a few years previously in America by a couple of twenty-two year old girls, Marianne Roney and Barbara Holdridge; the other, ARGO Records, was launched at about the same time in England by a leading young record producer called Harley Usill.

With its foundation Caedmon in effect led the way to creating and inspiring the whole spoken word recording industry. One of its earliest artists was Dylan Thomas, reciting extracts from *Under Milkwood*; ARGO fulfilled a long-held ambition of Harley Usill to record all the plays of Shakespeare with the finest casts in the world. He also produced notable renderings of choral works sung by the choir of King's College Cambridge.

ARGO's offices in Fulham Road were easier for me to get to than Caedmon's on the far side of the Atlantic, so I called Harley to arrange a meeting, and was invited to come over straight away.

He turned out to be an intense, likable man with a corrosive grudge: after a few years of joyous independence ARGO needed refinancing and Harley could not raise sufficient money. As a result he was forced to sell out to a much bigger record company, Decca. Decca gave him his head up to a point, but he had been downgraded from Chairman to Managing Director and was no longer his own master.

He therefore found it difficult to mention the name of Decca or its own founder, Sir Ted Lewis, who had successfully brought it to commercial maturity and stability, without bestowing an epithet. 'Bloody Decca' and 'that sod Lewis' were nearly always bracketed together.

However, Harley's permanent but fortunately latent anger didn't detract from his great charm and enthusiasm. He couldn't pay me much of a fee, he told me, but he liked the idea of the theatre record and if I could undertake to produce Coward and Ustinov he would do his best to get me some backing from 'bloody Decca'. Had I any idea how much Coward's or Ustinov's agents would demand in the way of payment?

I told him that neither agents nor payment had been mentioned, and that my impression was that both thought the record worth doing for its own sake.

Harley shook his head. "Good God, you think somebody's prepared to do something for nothing in this venal world? Most people think nothing is what something is worth, especially that bugger Lewis. Well well well! You might convince me yet that the world isn't entirely in the hands of shits! So who else do you see taking part?" he went on. "When you get two of the biggest names in

67

the world of theatre involved in a worthwhile project without a fee, others are going to feel privileged to join in. Or feel they'll have nothing to do with it out of envy, of course," he added.

"Well as Harold Pinter's just made a hell of an impression with The Caretaker at the Royal Court, and Osborne's done the same with Look Back in Anger over the past four years, I suggest we invite one of those. I saw The Caretaker last week and enjoyed it enormously, but God knows what it would have been like without Donald Pleasance."

"Happily we don't have to worry about what it would have been like without him. The fact is he's in it and is first rate in the part, thus putting Pinter in the spotlight."

I laughed and we spontaneously shook hands. My contract with ARGO would give me £300 on signature of contract, and when the finished record was marketed I would receive a modest royalty for each one sold. Although the contract might not be worth much in money terms the sense of achievement I felt in working with Coward, Ustinov and a top quality record company was fulfilling.

One of Ustinov's passions was tennis, and when I arrived at the Connaught for our interview he was fuming, because owing to a mix-up the big TV set on which he was looking forward to watching Wimbledon turned out to be a small and primitive set with a tiny screen, mounted on a trolley with a squeaky wheel. Nevertheless he concealed his wrath during our interview, his returned equanimity helped by the appearance of an assistant manager in tears with a passably up to date set with a large screen.

Ustinov not only talked extensively about the theatre, but also about every day personal experiences, which included being accosted everywhere by people recognising him. I remarked that that must drive him mad, and he admitted that it did.

"Until," he said, "I found myself one day stranded in Tirana. Nobody there knew me at all, and after twenty-four hours I was longing to be accosted." He gave a snorting laugh. "The most unusual act of recognition I ever experienced was in Hamburg, in the Herbertstrasse, off the Reperbahn. I was entertaining an opera director who had suffered some sort of mishap and needed to be cheered up, so I thought a night out on that particular part of the town would do him good.

"Outside two of the houses a couple of cages were hanging side by side. In the first was a colossal woman dressed all in leather and carrying a whip. She was in ardent conversation with an even bigger woman, dressed as a baby. She was in an immense nappy, and carrying a rattle the size of a marine mine. She caught sight of me standing, I must admit, with my mouth open—my friend too was in shock. The lady plunged a vast hand inside her pink outer garment and brought out an autograph book. 'Herr Ustinov?'

"I admitted my identity. 'Bitte, wollen Sie hier unterzeichen?' So I signed it for her and she replaced it between her copious breasts and went on chatting."

I found Ustinov exceedingly amiable; I was not quite sure of Coward's reaction to my Swiss visit. However, now that I had established some sort of professional identity with ARGO I felt far more confident than before in going to Switzerland for lunch and an in-depth interview with the Master. Unfortunately, that confidence was to last only until Geneva, when it was replaced by shock.

In order to avoid the considerable extra baggage charge and inconvenience of saddling myself with a BBC EMI tape recorder, I arranged with CBC to pick up a tape-recorder at their Geneva offices early on Saturday morning on the way to catch the train to Montreux.

When I arrived there was only one person on duty in Reception: he was a Swiss of German derivation whose tongue was Schweitzer

Standarddeutsch, a passable imitation of what a cat would sound like if it spat in German.

After several attempts I managed to pierce his clouded comprehension as to what I wanted and my name, and he gave a little snort of triumph and went over to a cupboard. Taking something from inside, he brought it to where I was standing. There was a label with my name tied to its handle, and to my dismay and disbelief something like a miniature starting handle was taped to its top. Somebody had selected an old wind-up recorder for me to interview one of the most exigent and sophisticated actors in the world.

In a lowering state of nightmare, I picked up the Nagra, as the recorder was called, with its microphone and cable lying in an untidy coil like an extinct ratsnake, and took a cab to the station. I was still in a state of shock as I climbed into the train and tried to settle calmly into a first class compartment. I knew it would be impossible to maintain the recording speed of the Nagra absolutely constant; Coward's uniquely pitched voice would swing from tenor to base as the spring uncoiled and I could imagine the sort of ruthless mockery I would have to undergo. The only thing to do with the Nagra was to hurl it out of the window and buy something that worked by electricity, but I was on a moving train halfway up an Alp.

I changed trains at Lausanne and the gradient of the track became steeper. Big wooden houses gleamed with the pale lustre of deer through dark green pines, and I remembered the comments of my mother's sister Sandra, after trying to find a finishing school in Switzerland for my cousin Julia. "How I loathe pseudo-intellectual antiquity: it produces dangerously dry wood and varnish when the aim of a finishing school should be to produce polish."

The moment I was dreading arrived as we stopped in Montreux station. I reluctantly picked up the recorder and took a taxi to the Palace Hotel, where I was booked to stay.

A grandly uniformed porter stretched out a white-gloved hand to take the Nagra; partly out of shame I clung to it and offered him my blue overnight bag as a substitute.

The lobby was full of discreet gold-lettered signs and accompanying directional arrows, proclaiming that the BBC's first Golden Rose Festival was being celebrated in the hotel ballroom. I peered disbelievingly at the display inside.

The ballroom was filled with tables under glistening white cloths, and on the cloths were dozens of state-of-the-art tape-recorders. They shone with showroom splendour—Ampex, EMI, Ficord, Sony, Philips, Nagra. There wasn't a wind-up among the lot.

The man at the Nagra table had recognised the antique model I was carrying, and came hurrying towards me. He was slender and nearly bald and had exceptionally bright and intelligent eyes.

"A wind-up!" he exclaimed, "my first model. It's so good to see it again. I have been wanting one of these for my museum collection!"

"I'll swap it for one of those," I said jokingly. I wasn't joking. I gestured at the machines laid out on display. "I have to go and interview Noël Coward this afternoon."

He laughed. "But of course." He picked up a tape recorder and placed it beside me before taking the wind-up from my hands as tenderly as a mother reaching out to the midwife for her first sight of her newborn.

"The wind-up was a good machine in its day, but its day has been over for some time." He nodded at the one he had put beside me. "One day that one too will be obsolete, but for the time being it is safe to say that nothing will give a better recording."

I thanked him again for rescuing me from my predicament.

"I am delighted to be of help. As there is not much time before you are due at Noël Coward's let me show you how the Nagra works. It is quite simple."

71

Usually that phrase is to me the kiss of death, but the Nagra really was easy to operate, and it was light to carry and aesthetically pleasing.

My saviour was a young Polish inventor called Stefan Kudelski, who called his product Nagra because it means in Polish 'will record'. He told me he had been born in Warsaw in 1929 and had an active childhood with his family managing to keep ahead of the Nazis; the Kudelskis fled from Poland to Hungary successfully and thence to Switzerland, where Stefan completed his technical studies as an electronic engineer.

"A Nagra, eh? My God you fell on your feet," a technical correspondent for a weekly magazine said later than evening. "They're the best in the world."

"I don't know about falling on *my* feet, I answered, "I think I fell on Stefan Kudelski's."

After my brief induction course I sat in the back of the taxi on the way to Montreux-les-Avants, high above the sleek lakeside city of its namesake and the distant mirror of Lake Leman. I rested my hand on the Nagra's warm metal top in a conscious blessing, still hardly able to believe it was mine and at last feeling anticipation rather than dread of the interview.

Below the floor of the veranda on which Coward, his secretary Cole Leslie and friend Graham Payn—for whom he allegedly wrote *Mad About The Boy*—a platoon of cows was dreamily contributing to the pastoral scene, cowbells clanking gently as they ruminated. Even more musical was the sound of the ice in our glasses, handed round by a handsome, rococo-buttocked Italian boy.

Coward and Leslie wore open-necked, short-sleeved shirts, whilst Payn sported a blazer as well and looked rather like a cricketer in a Rattigan play about a country house weekend. The staging might have been deliberate, as Rattigan was Coward's favourite modern playwright.

Over lunch, I asked Coward if a story I had heard about him was true or apocryphal.

"A cub reporter from the Sunday Pictorial is alleged to have tried to barge his way into your cabin aboard the Queen Mary for an interview. He was so persistent when you tried to throw him out you agreed to answer just one question, which was: "what do you think of Hollywood, Mr. Coward?"

"And what did I answer?"

I did my best to imitate Coward's inimitable voice: "Hollywood is a place where some people lie on the beach and look up at the stars, whereas other people lie on the stars and look down at the beach."

I was surprised and gratified at the immediate shout of laughter: it is normally impossible to tell someone a personal anecdote who hasn't heard it dozens of times before.

After lunch Coward led the way into the library and spoke for forty minutes and almost without a pause into the microphone. It was, like all his performances, impeccable, and so was that of the Nagra.

"I wanted to be a star," he began, "and to be recognised in public. In fact, I get rather cross with stars who rush out of the stage door with handkerchiefs over their faces because they don't want to be recognised." He used an unusual form of phraseology. "If you want to be a star you must take it on the jaw and go on giving a performance until you get safely home behind locked doors."

This seemed to imply that actors acted all the time and regarded home as a refuge, outside which they were constantly under siege. However, I was sure Coward's natural loftiness prevented him from suffering much in the way of siege syndrome.

He went on to talk with scorn of actors who asked about the 'motivation' of the character. "The answer to that, of course, is your pay cheque at the end of the week. If an actor told me he felt the same emotions playing a part six times a week and two matinees I wouldn't believe him anyway."

When I arrived back at the Palace Stefan Kudelski came up to me to ask how things had gone and I embraced him like a brother. "Would you like to listen to the quality of your machine's performance, Stefan?"

"Very much." I handed him the tape, and soon Coward's tones danced through the ballroom. "The prime purpose of the theatre has always been to me, to entertain, although of course I'm not infallible and I might be quite, quite wrong."

Several hotel guests drifted into the ballroom to listen, including the ineffably named Daily Telegraph correspondent L. Marsland Gander, who had the same sort of querulous outlook on life as W.C. Fields, and was extremely droll without meaning to be.

I came across him the next morning in the hotel car park, almost incoherent with rage, surrounded by amused journalists as he peered into the bonnet of his hired Volkswagen.

"Some bastard's pinched the engine!" he howled, looking like a distressed heron. "Bastards!"

"It's all right, Marsland, the engine's at the back," somebody assured him. "It's a Volkswagen. That's where the engine is supposed to be. Nobody's stolen anything."

"Not much of a motoring correspondent, are you Marsland?" someone else said mischievously.

"I'm not a bloody motoring correspondent!" as there was another shout of laughter. Still unconvinced that the front part of the car was the baggage space, Gander lifted the boot lid and glared at the engine. "Stupid bloody place to put an engine," he said. He flung open the front compartment, hurled his suitcase inside and slammed the bonnet.

With more laughter at his expense, we dispersed.

CHAPTER TWELVE

"Walter, I'm getting married soon and I need a flat. Is there an empty one in your building, by any chance? They're damn difficult to find in Central London." Dick Francis and I were having a drink in a West End Bar after a meeting at Lime Grove with Wednesday Magazine's producer, Lorna Pegram.

"I could have a word with Sansom, our Head Porter. Do I know your bride?" I asked.

"Yes. Beata Harnisch. We had a drink in the Crown and Two Chairmen the other evening."

"The girl from Hamburg? I didn't think you knew her that well."

"We're getting to know each other better by the day. It isn't a *grande passion* yet, but I'm not sure such a thing exists anyway.. Even if it does things are bound to settle down in a marriage after a while. You can't maintain a level of romance at full blast for long— so far as I'm concerned, serenity is more important than passion anyway when it comes to setting out on a career as well as building a marriage."

"Don't you think you're being perhaps too cold-blooded about it? Bea might want to be wooed passionately."

"I'm not being cold-blooded, simply logical."

"All right, I'll have a word with Sansom—if there is a flat going you'll probably have to go through the usual minor venalities of slipping a tenner or so into his hand."

"That's fine. I'm sorry I can't invite you to the wedding, but it's Bea's parents who are paying for it so I feel I should keep the cost down."

Sansom was skinny and grey, and had chipolata lips which were designed for morose sucking, accompanied by an intake of breath and a negative shake of the head when he was asked to do something, weighed it in the balance and found it wanting. This performance meant he might oblige if he was persuaded by an increase in the gratuity on offer.

When I asked him if there was an empty flat available for some friends of mine offering a finder's fee of £20, Dick and Bea were installed on the floor below mine within a couple of weeks. Almost immediately they got married and went on honeymoon.

Three evenings later, I received a phone call from Bea, asking me to go down at once to see her. She sounded in a lachrymose, cry on shoulder mood, and I hoped it wasn't mine that was going to get wet. I assured her I would be right down.

When I arrived she was already standing in the corridor, with the anxious face of someone waiting for a bus on a rainy night—how long would it be, would it bring deliverance soon, had the service been suspended? She let me in and shut the front door, whereupon she hurried back to the crumpled marital bed and resumed crying.

Sitting awkwardly in a chair whose bow legs reminded me of Charles Chaplin when he was still Charlie the tramp, I wondered how on earth to comfort an upset bride. Perhaps finding out what had happened to the groom would be a start.

"Where's Dick?" I asked.

She let loose the sobs she had been holding in reserve. "He's shooting!"

"Shooting? What on earth is he shooting?"

"A bloody documentary about Cornwall! That's where we've been on honeymoon!"

"Oh." It was neither comment nor consolation, I suppose, but I had been caught short on the conversational front.

77

"He told me he wouldn't give anyone the number of our hotel and then gave it to the producer of Wednesday Magazine. I picked up the phone and said we weren't taking any calls because we were on honeymoon and the bitch said: 'He'll take this one! Tell him it's Lorna.' I don't suppose she's ever been on honeymoon herself!"

I knew Lorna. She was inclined to be peremptory and intolerant of mistakes, which was possibly how she viewed Dick's and Beata's nuptial liaison. "She does tend to get straight to the point," I said.

"You know her?" There was a flash of hostility through the tears and I hastily told Bea that I had only met Lorna once or twice. Anticipating her following question: what did Lorna look like? I pursed my lips and adopted a doubtful expression, indicating that no man in his right mind would go within a mile of her. As she was actually quite good-looking I mentally apologised to her for the silent slander.

"Dick's very professional," I ploughed on, "I'm sure he had no intention of hurting you."

"When he comes back I shall tell him I do not like him to be too professional."

"I really wouldn't advise that, Bea. You should never use a word as an insult which is usually regarded as a compliment."

To my relief she sat upright and wiped her eyes. "Thank you, you have been very helpful. I shall not insult him this time."

I gave her an indulgent smile which probably looked as false as it was. "Well, it's a bit early in your marriage for insults. I'm sure Dick didn't mean to upset you," I assured her again.

"I do not want him to put work before me," she repeated: "I do not want him to be too much professional."

Impatience with her made me tactless. "Bea, play it like a Frenchwoman. Put your arms round his neck, kiss him and tell him how pleased you are he's back and that you missed him."

"But I am not French. I am German."

I stopped a heavy sigh just in time. "Excuse me, Bea, I have to go back upstairs to take a phone call."

I took my leave, wondering what odds a bookie would give on the marriage lasting six months, and decided that the likely offer would hardly be worth the bet.

CHAPTER THIRTEEN

The radio producer John Bridges, whom Dick Francis was originally hired to assist, commissioned me to do my first BBC interview in 1958. There were two major radio wave lengths—the Home Service, which catered for more serious tastes, and the Light Programme, which was more at home with frivolity. John Bridges was responsible for a Light Programme offering, *Saturday Night on the Light*, or more colloquially by its anagram *SNOL*.

In an industry founded only thirty-six years previously, John had become one of the old school of producer, dressing rather like a prep school master of the day in tweed jacket with leather elbow pads, light grey trousers, and of course a tie. He had rather bulbous blue eyes that looked as perpetually resentful as a chihuahua's and a belief that mistakes should be punished appropriately, as I soon found out.

The British Grand Prix at Silverstone was the next race on the calendar, and I asked John to commission me to interview some drivers at the track. He consented.

"If you can interview the winner and get back here in time, we might scoop the news and sports boys by airing your piece on the programme."

I thanked him and said I would do my best to get back in time.

In one respect, Silverstone has changed little over the decades: there are only two ways to escape the intense traffic leaving after the Grand Prix. One is to arrive by air, the other to leave before the end of the race.

The pit lane was filled with noise and activity, a crèche of racing cars each being nourished at a teat yielding one hundred and thirty octane petrol, or when their appetites were satisfied coughing and roaring in an effort to get attention.

The air was also raw with the strangely beguiling smell of Castrol; the cars' exhausts smelled just as they had during my childhood visits to Brooklands and, in 1937, my first Grand Prix, won by the red-helmeted German driver Count von Brautschitch in a Mercedes Benz at Monaco.

Stirling Moss walked towards me and I caught his eye and asked him some questions about motor racing and his personal experiences. His answers were concise, humorous and to the point, giving me a pleasantly lucid interview.

After him Michael Hawthorn and Peter Collins approached, chatting together. They reminded me of World War Two fighter pilots, merry, carefree and charming. Like those pilots, they lived lives which could be appallingly brief. They were not interested in giving me a serious or coherent interview, and continued on their way, laughing and joking, two blonde young men drawn to classical Greek God specifications but denied immortality.

The race started, and Stirling Moss's name came frequently over the splutter of the amplifiers—he was in the lead and stayed there. I thought of the possibilities of a scoop, and the pleasure of announcing Stirling's victory before anyone else. Stirling remained in the lead and there were only a few laps to go till the chequered flag. I decided to take a chance and leave shortly before the race ended.

When I arrived at Broadcasting House a few minutes before the start of SNOL, John Bridges was standing on the steps, smoking a pipe. "Good timing," he said. "Did you get the winner?"

"Yes. I got a good interview with Stirling Moss."

"That's not what I asked. Did you get the winner?"

I felt my mouth fall open. "But Stirling—"

"Peter Collins was the winner, in a Ferrari 246."

"Oh God." I felt as much of a fool as a fraud.

John gave me his most bulbous-eyed Chichuahua glare. "Well, I'll tell you what I'm going to do. I'm going to put you on air live to explain to our listeners how you failed to interview the winner of the 1958 Silverstone Grand Prix. Come on."

I never took a winner for granted again, till he had been given the chequered flag. A few days later I was glad in a way that Peter Collins had triumphed; he was killed in his very next championship race, the German Grand Prix.

CHAPTER FOURTEEN

In 1956 the publication of Gerald Durrell's first book, *My Family And Other Animals*, launched it on its way to becoming Durrell's best-known book and one of the most loved in the English language (and no doubt in others).

All his books were infused with humour although, like Sir David Attenborough, he was deadly serious about the perils of extinction facing so many species as a result of the over-multiplication, ruthlessness and egocentricity of the human race.

One of the reasons Gerald (who preferred to be called Gerry) had founded his own zoo, Les Augrès, was the pain he felt at having to sell animals he had personally collected and in some cases hand-reared, for other zoos, another was his feeling that many species were in danger of extinction, and that the best way to ensure their survival was to establish a zoo with the facilities to breed them in captivity.

Les Augrès had been a Jersey manor house, and was converted into a zoo incorporating Gerry's ideas of how a zoo should be designed and run. CBC enthusiastically agreed with my suggestion that I should go to interview him at Les Augrès, and I arrived as he was having a conversation with a caged black bear. It was trying to reach him through the bars, but with affectionate rather than gastronomic intent.

"Yes, I know you love me," he crooned, making sure he was out of reach of the claws just behind. "I love you too, but I can't stay with you now, because I have another engagement. Some other time, darling."

We set off on a tour of the zoo, in a manner which reminded me of the Queen holding a summer garden party. The animals and birds all behaved like subjects wanting to be noticed; some postured politely but with a show of determined ostentation, others caught Gerry's eye and couldn't constrain themselves from greeting him, whilst he chatted to them in gracious acknowledgement.

The zoo was constructed on the open air and space principle, the separation of visitor and resident being as unobtrusive as possible. A ditch the size of a large medieval moat was all that prevented contact between humans and animals, and I reflected that a ballister would be a perfect engine for firing projectiles of protein across it to a couple of lionesses yawning in the sun like heraldic beasts come to life.

Gerry had of course drawn on his own immense experience of zoos, and most of the animals he had brought back from the wild for sale had found homes in such progressive sanctuaries as Whipsnade, New York's Bronx Zoo, and the Hagenbeck Zoo, founded in Hamburg by Carl Hagenbeck the enlightened son and namesake of a Hamburg fishmonger who began collecting and displaying wild animals in 1863.

I was introduced to a pair of mongooses named Tikki and Tavi, which had come from the Cameroon territory presided over by the Fon of Bafut, who made his Falstaffian appearance in another joyous book by Gerald Durrell, *The Bafut Beagles.*

Gerry was appalled at first at the book's effect on the life of the Fon, a previously unknown ruler of a land which had once been a German colony in West Africa.

He was reassured however by the immense pleasure the Fon found in his new status as a cynosure of hospitality and entertainment, and the compliment his visitors paid him of undergoing long and complicated journeys for the pleasure of his company.

Gerry's tribute to the Fon's capacity for alcohol was interrupted by a splendidly plumed bird which could have been an ornithological incarnation of the Fon except that it was relatively sober. It did a fluttering dance round Gerry whilst addressing him with excruciating shrieks and a loud, clattering combination of its beak and thorax.

We moved on, and he told me how peoples' imaginations sometimes gave them the wrong idea about a creature's characteristics. "For example, owls have a reputation for being wise, but in fact they're brainless." He particularly liked the small burrowing owls of Argentina, which lived in holes in the ground.

"One thing which does give me encouragement about the future is the questions people ask about animals these days. They used to be imbecilic—for example, what is that deer for? Of course, the only answer to that is: 'What are *you* for?'"

He thought that Walt Disney had had a beneficent effect, particularly on children. "Children are much less likely to grow up into hunters after seeing Bambi. There's all that sentimentality too, of course, but on the whole Disney's been a good influence."

It was as a result of visiting Gerry that I was shortly to do a television interview on Wednesday Magazine with his brother Lawrence.

It is said that we forget pain and remember pleasure, which is not, I soon discovered, always the case.

CHAPTER FIFTEEN

I was pretty sure that Lawrence Durrell, a notoriously shy man, would not have agreed to my interviewing him on *Wednesday Magazine* without the urging of Claire, his French wife, and Gerry. Lawrence had for years been working on four major novels set in Alexandria, and collectively referred to as *The Alexandrian Quartet*. Their individual titles were exotic and redolent of the history and atmosphere of modern Alexandria: *Justine; Balthazar; Mountolive* and *Clea*. They had been published in sequence during the late fifties, and I would be interviewing Lawrence in 1962 on the eve of publication of the whole Quartet simultaneously. This I regarded as a feather in my interviewing cap, but of course it is not only the feather but its colour which matters. I thought in terms of humming birds, but the feather the fates had chosen for my cap was the colour of a raven's.

Lawrence and I greeted each other at the porter's lodge at Lime Grove and climbed the chilly concrete staircase leading to the various studios and sets. Wednesday Magazines's was uncluttered, as I recall; the producer Lorna Pegram, who had so offended Beata, operated from a recording booth which like so much else at Lime Grove breathed an aura of antiquity which would have made Tutankhamun feel at home.

A well-known broadcaster of the day, Robert Kee, tall and sleek, had already had his equanimity disturbed by the news that the person he was interviewing was stranded in Holland because of poor visibility at Schipol Airport—I believe he was a schoolboy but can't remember what the interview was supposed to be about.

Videos, smartphones and the whole vast miscellany of today's equipment, whose sole purpose is not so much to enable us to remember as to make it impossible to forget, had yet to be invented. Few programmes were even recorded, and any mistake was impossible to rectify and went out live, providing the viewer with extra if unscheduled entertainment.

Dick Francis joined Lorna in her booth and Lawrence and I were already fidgeting, he because of the delay and I because I hadn't had the time or opportunity to read the Alexandrian Quartet and was joining him in his mounting apprehension.

These days, it is possible in a few minutes to learn from the Internet the gist of anything or anyone one is researching; in 1962 the best information available was in the nearest public library, which usually closed soon after the librarian had siphoned down her final cup of afternoon tea.

Given that I am a fairly quick reader, the Quartet would probably have taken me at least a couple of months to get through, but I had had only twenty-four hours notification of Lawrence's arrival and couldn't find a copy. The only work of his I could lay my hands on was *Bitter Lemons*, reviewed I recall as a travel book and dealing principally with the civil war in Cyprus. I had spent most of the night absorbing its irrelevance, so that I was having to pretend to Lawrence that I was wide awake, when my eyelids felt like metal shutters about to slam shut. The name that kept nibbling at my mind was not Balthazar but Makarios, the rogue archbishop supporting Cyprus's Greek rebels.

Dick came over to tell us we could leave the set for ten minutes for relief and refreshment; we couldn't have a proper break until the stranded schoolboy showed up. Robert Kee seemed to have entered the comatose realm of a man who has had more anti-climaxes than he can bear, which of course always leaves the last one. He was sitting on a chair and holding a newspaper as he stared fixedly at a lifeless camera. Someone with a beard was being examined by a trio of cameras one after the other, as he juggled a pair of newts in a tank and discoursed learnedly on frog-sperm.

Lorna beckoned me over to tell me that Lawrence and I would be on air in five minutes, and mentioned something about 'over-rehearsing' and how we had had too much time together to convey the necessary spontaneity to the interview. The missing schoolboy's scheduled appearance on the programme was going to be postponed, so we would be the next item to go out.

I did my best to convince Lawrence that it was an achievement for us to be rescheduled, but I could tell by his pallor that he didn't believe me. He was terrified, and I was far from sanguine that his fear wouldn't prove contagious. Even if he didn't dry up, there seemed a good chance that I might.

Desperately, I tried to infuse the dying interview with some sort of spark, but couldn't even manage an ember. A few uninspired questions about the time and effort my guest had put into writing the Alexandrian Quartet and if its characters were based on people he had known, was the best I could do, by which time Lawrence's eyes had acquired the glaze of a crystallised pear.

As we both dried up completely, Dick semaphored with his hands and Lorna mouthed oaths through the glass of her booth.

I thanked Lawrence for his time and wished his books success and the camera's red Polyphemus eye went out. Dick called a taxi for him and held open the door whilst he struggled to climb inside and banged his head on the roof. He leaned forward and croaked an address to the driver, failing to smile a farewell at me as he collapsed on to the back seat.

"Well, you can't win them all," said Dick, in a tone indicating that he didn't believe what he was saying.

Lorna was a little more sympathetic, but not much. Current affairs TV may have gone out live, but my Lawrence interview had shown no sign of life. I hadn't thought on my feet and I had failed to offer any stimulus to the programme. What was more, I showed no sign of having researched my subject.

Dick was absent when I left the building. I had fouled up; for the time being at least I was not a suitable person for him to associate with.

I never did a television interview again.

CHAPTER SIXTEEN

Theatre 60 was progressing quite well; I invited Kenneth Tynan to represent critics and Ustinov remarked with caustic elegance that "critics are critics because they're so much more intelligent than we are." Peter Hall was already a distinguished producer-director in his early twenties when he contributed, and our set designer Sean Kenny was an inventive and original Irish architect who had been responsible for the set of Lionel Bart's *Oliver!* and the same playwright's *Blitz!*

I had interviewed Sean Kenny in Peter Cook's office in his Establishment Club in Soho. Eventually Peter Cook married his widow.

As there were nine interviews to edit I introduced Dick Francis and Harley, who agreed that Dick should have the overall titles of producer and editor. I wrote the sleeve notes, including the story of how the record came to be made, and carried on as usual providing interviews which went out on *The Today Programme* and CBC'S *Assignment* slot. One of the interviews was with Bing Crosby at a private room at the Lotus House after he had finished dinner; Johnnie Koon tipped me off he was there and would see me so long as I didn't let on about his presence; he wasn't wearing his customary hairpiece and looked quite different from himself in movies. The girl he was with looked like his wife Dixie Lee, but wasn't.

On the eve of the premier of *On The Alamo* John Wayne accepted my invitation to be interviewed. I knew the personification of this strong, silent man of the West—whether playing a sheriff, cowboy, ranch owner or soldier—was personally interested in politics and whose sympathies were very right wing. Concealing my own satisfaction that the Democrat Kennedy had beaten the Republican

Nixon in the recent Presidential elections, I listened happily to Wayne's expressions of displeasure at the result.

By doing so, and then getting Wayne to talk about horses and the stunt men who rode them (it was they who got hurt or occasionally killed) Wayne himself said he had never come across a stunt-damaged horse. I managed to turn the interview into a talk with a real person with likes, dislikes and prejudices, instead of simply being awarded a first night puff.

However, I accidentally started a running gaffe at the outset, when I asked Wayne what I should call him; most stars liked to be addressed by their first names or nicknames.

Hindsight assured me he had asked to be addressed as 'Duke' which doubtless had the sort of Wellingtonian resonance he felt he deserved, but unfortunately that wasn't what I heard. The result was that the *Today Programme* went out the following morning carrying the name of a new Western star called 'Dude' Wayne.

I thought the interview also demonstrated how taciturn the strong, silent men of the Old West—so often portrayed by John Wayne—really were, and how difficult to deal with. If one's fate was to die young, maybe it was perhaps preferable to be shot rather than bored.

CHAPTER SEVENTEEN

I knew that Dick Francis was interested in making some TV documentary episodes for *Wednesday Magazine* and suggested that Morocco might be an enjoyable and interesting venue to carry out the project. I happened to be friendly with the Moroccan travel attaché in London, Laby Barada, a bat-eared little man with merry eyes and a tall White Russian wife called Eugenia who knew that, if ever Laby wanted to replace her, he could do so under Islamic law by simply going into his local mosque and announcing: "I divorce thee" three times. Under contemporary Moroccan legislation, Laby's travel section at the Moroccan Embassy was a Moroccan Government agency, giving him official status; he could thus open doors for us all over his country. Dick was going to direct on behalf of the BBC, a friend of mine called Bob Angell,whom I had first met at Montreux, was going to produce under the aegis of his production company, Puritan Films, and I was going as sound man and interpreter. The cameraman would be a member of BBC TV staff

"Of course, you know who you are in my country, don't you Walter?" Laby asked over dinner.

"?"

"You are a hero, and will be treated like one."

"Er, how is that, Laby?"

Instead of answering directly, he told me the story of an Englishman called Walter Burton Harris. He was affluent and a homosexual; having failed, not surprisingly, to consummate the marriage he contracted soon after leaving Harrow School, he had applied for its annulment and in 1886, at the age of 19, arrived in the accommodatingly decadent city of Tangier, where he built a sumptuous villa.

With a light brown skin and a gift for languages, including Arabic, Harris was able to disguise himself as a Moroccan bandit and travel to parts of Morocco unavailable to other non-Arabs to explore. In fact there were parts of the country such as the Rif Mountains where, until the mid-twenties, anyone who was not a Muslim could have his throat cut for being an Unbeliever.

Harris joined The Times as its Moroccan correspondent, and was also attached as a diplomat to the staff of the British Embassy in Rabat, Morocco's capital. His unorthodox and original approach to a country which had been established as a going pirate concern nearly five hundred years previously also stood him in good stead; the highly profitable activities of the Corsairs of the Barbary Coast, most of whose delinquents were Berbers (hence the name) had evolved into a political shambles.

In 1912, the Sultan lost power to the Spanish and French, and the Rif rebel Abd el-Krim eventually rebelled a decade later, deciding to seize back the former Spanish enclaves of Ceuta and Medilla. Walter Harris went to investigate and Abd el-Krim kidnapped him.

A large ransom was demanded and paid, but Harris did not return. The British sent an expeditionary force to rescue him, only to find him playing cards for the ransom money with his captor.

"I wonder how I'd have behaved in his place, Laby."

Laby shrugged. "Probably not like him, but that doesn't stop you being a hero in Morocco's eyes. Whatever you do, don't admit you are not related to the man you are not related to. You will cause only disappointment and gain nothing." He gently patted my shoulder. "And now let us arrange a meeting with your friends and plan your itinerary."

We were not told that the itinerary was to take place during the *Fête de Mouton*, when sheep were worn across men's shoulders like shawls and sacrificed in the courtyards of the rich. However Laby had arranged for us to be merely dipped into Moroccan culture rather than deep-ended, so after a pleasant flight to Tangier via Gibraltar we spent the night at the Rif Hotel, which was situated on the sea front and gently cast its ambience of luxury into the ozone whilst a dozen horses attached to calèches sulked nearby as they peered over feedbags.

In front of the Rif its manager, a jolly, personable man called David Safarti, had parked his brand new Mercedes Benz 300SL. Inside the hotel he had prepared a welcoming banquet for us. "My friend Mr Barada has requested it especially," he told us.

Next morning, the professionalism of each of us—including Dick—marred by a hangover, we set off in our hired car with Bob at the wheel, along the coast road leading from Tangier to Tetouan, where the road began to twist and turn its upward way through the foothills of the Rif Mountains. Our destination was the once sacred city of Xaouan, which had been the hold-out and fief of Abd el-Krim. We were to be the luncheon guests of the Basha—Deputy Governor—of Xaouan, and to present our compliments to him when we arrived.

On the way, we stopped for refreshment; Dick, Bob and John the cameraman decided to have another glass of mint tea, and I wandered through a small market-place to record the sounds of Arab bargaining. There were sheep everywhere, and as I lugged the tape recorder through the place, I became aware that it was being eyed by the muttering locals with increasing hostility, which focused on me as well. I headed back to the tea-shop, wishing I could enjoy a reincarnation of some of Walter Burton Harris's diplomatic abilities, and tried to look casual. At least Safarti's gift of a severe hangover had gone.

The Basha was holding a *diwan* when we arrived, a Court of Justice set up here and there for his subjects as he travelled the region rather in the style of a Circuit Judge. He considered petitions, was the ultimate arbiter in disputes and helped in the solution of people's personal difficulties which might otherwise have festered into resentment. A queue of people waiting their turn to see him stretched into the distance.

I was directed by an official to go straight in. A well-upholstered, imperious Moroccan in robes sat flanked by evidently lesser dignitaries.

I greeted him in Spanish, calling him Your Excellency, which may not always be accurate but never offends, and presented the BBC's compliments. When I introduced myself, he leaped to his feet and embraced me, whilst the other dignitaries regarded me with expressions of mingled awe and delight. My name did seem to trigger special respect.

"Venga almuezar comigo en mi casa a una hora!" I thanked the Basha for his invitation and went outside into the street. Nobody in the queue complained about my gate-crashing and in fact nobody seemed to have moved an inch.

"We've been invited to the Basha's house for lunch at one," I told my colleagues. "Here's the address," handing over a pencil scrawl one of the dignitaries had given me.

"Well, I suppose we'll have time for a quick sandwich," said Dick, "which will give us plenty of time to shoot afterwards. I'm glad your Spanish came in useful, Walter."

"I don't think the Basha said anything about sandwiches."

"Well, whatever's on the menu needn't take us long. We've had a look round," he went on, "and the mountain meadows look pretty

95

scenic. There are assherds going up and down with various animals—donkeys, sheep, goats—so we should have a productive afternoon."

"Good," I said.

It turned out that the Basha had other ideas. He had put on western clothing, and introduced us in perfectly good English to his other guests, who included an Arabic-speaking man with a jovial laugh and probing eyes who was announced as being the region's East German Chief of Police. Apparently he had once held this position in the Sans Souci district of Potsdam. There were several other guests, and we were invited to lower ourselves on to thick cushions. When we had managed this, which depending on one's shape required squatting skill, the Basha clapped his hands and a girl with henna'd hands came in carrying a heavy tray of beaten bronze. Across it sprawled an extensive tableau of kidneys, liver and fried eggs. The girl managed to lower the dish on to a low table, and we all went to work trying to eat.

The art of eating fried eggs with one's fingers was, I found, not easily acquired, and the further acquisition of greasy chops, which fell frequently into my lap but not my mouth, was hardly nourishing. It took ages to feel one had eaten anything at all, and I was still hungry when the Basha clapped his hands and the girl came in with the next course, another bronze dish weighted with chops, legs, and shoulders of lamb. I braced myself for the presentation of sheep's eyes, but mercifully it didn't occur.

The meal ended with a paddling pool-sized dish filled with oranges and pomegranates.

"We eat a lot of lamb and mutton in this country, especially at this time of year," the Basha told us.

Dick wiped his mouth on a sheet masquerading as a napkin. "What will you have for dinner tonight, Your Excellency?"

96

"The same as for lunch, but starting from the outside. One likes a little variety."

I turned to the police chief, who asked me how my morning's recording in the market had gone.

"I'm not sure. People didn't seem too happy about it."

"May I listen?"

"Of course."

"Do you speak Arabic?"

"I'm afraid not. Would you mind translating?"

"With pleasure."

I switched the machine on and voices filled the room, muttering and displeased.

The Basha laughed loudly and clapped his hands, inadvertently once more summoning the serving girl.

"What are they saying?" I asked.

The police chief too could hardly speak for laughing. "They are saying why is this fucking foreigner stealing our souls with his evil eye? They think your recorder is a camera, which will steal the essence of themselves, their souls."

It was mid-afternoon when we finally left the Basha's residence; he insisted on giving us an armed escort, a villainous-looking man wearing a military képi and a crossover necklace of cartridges. When Dick pointed at an assherd and a dozen goats coming down the hillside, the guard rushed at him and shouted to him to go back up the mountain immediately or be shot.

"Not very helpful," commented Dick, watching the drama through his view-finder. The assherd scrambled back to an upper slope, obviously bemused and wondering what he had done wrong.

"The assherd's bleeding," said Bob, "I think the gendarme gave him a clout with his rifle-butt. A generous tip is called for, but not in view of the gendarme."

When we had finished the shoot we dropped our escort in the centre of the city, looking down from a terrace at a meeting place below, where people strolled about chatting and donkeys with panniers squeezed their way up and down narrow flights of steps, the men riding, the women walking behind them, just as they had doubtless walked through the centuries.

After Xouan we shot another episode in the ancient city of Fez, where Laby had arranged for us what he called an 'entertainment'. This turned out to be the sacrifice of a ram in the courtyard of an affluent family, who watched the proceedings from the roof.

After being sprayed with rosewater, Bob, Dick and I averted our eyes as the animal was led into the courtyard by a butcher in robes and ceremonial hat. He carried a scimitar. John stood behind his camera, the only one of the four of us who had no option but to watch the proceedings attentively and make sure the British viewers didn't miss anything they could stomach.

We heard the ram fall over and the drumming of its hooves on the ground; I turned my head towards the proceedings and saw the butcher make an incision into one of the poor beast's rear legs and breathe into it so that it swelled up. I think the idea was to speed the blood flow from its throat and the separation of the fat from the flesh. The tattoo of hooves accelerated, and then were still.

The butcher removed the dead ram from the courtyard and we sighed with relief that the ordeal, both for us and the ram, was over, but because our hosts had to demonstrate their affluence another butcher led a second ram into view.

If Walter Harris wanted to be a hero, giving way to nausea at a simple ovine sacrifice wasn't the way to go about it. Thankfully, I found an old peppermint in the pocket of my shorts and synchronised my chewing with the fresh drumming of hooves which had just started in front of us.

We thanked our hosts for their offer of hospitality—I saw one of the butchers towing his newly-killed sheep to the kitchen door—and hurried out of range, first for a look at Fez's ancient and impressive Keraouine Mosque, and then witnessing a *fantasia,* a frightening gallop through the city's narrow alleys and sun-toasted pastures on the backs of camels, horses and donkeys, the jockeys shouting, waving rifles and firing into the air as the wind plucked savagely at their flowing robes, caftans and turbans.

Unlike the Lawrence Durrell interview, the Moroccan episodes added something to BBC daylight television, as did another three a few months later which made up a documentary we shot in Holland.

The first episode was a trip out to sea aboard a Dutch fishing-boat, and the second a visit to an attractive village called Gjiethorn, which was girded by streams and river banks on which clusters of girls lay on their backs, shading their eyes from the sun as they lowered eels down their throats in priapic abandon. Our third sequence was devoted to the city of Delft.

Delft fulfils one's desire for colour with its delicate porcelain blue, a blue and white city permeated by the sound as well as the sight of blue when the firm chimes of its church clocks stride through the soft evening that moulds the ambience of its market square.

The music of Dutch clocks chiming is quite different from English ones. They perform in a different key that summons up portraits by Breughel of black and white interiors smelling of the past, of Huguenot weavers and Volendam pickled herrings and Rembrandt peering into his mirror as he painted his own portrait and reminisced with the outer limits of his imagination. Dutch clocks use chimes in conversation as Rembrandt painted light.

Holland is as flat as Morocco is mountainous, and its clocks are its version of the muezzins of the evening. Morocco breathes with the neurotic excitement of latent violence but manages to smile at those benevolent intruders who wish to explore it. Holland folds its arms and placidly smiles at the world as the clocks gently converse across its dykes and polders.

Opposite Amsterdam's Lido is an art nouveau hotel called the Hotel Americain. Bob, Dick, and John had gone to the Rijksmuseum which I had visited a couple of months previously on another trip to Holland, so I decided to have a drink in the 1930s bar and inhale the Americain's atmosphere.

Shortly after I had ordered, a man came in wearing a camel hair coat and carrying a dog lead. He sat down at a table nearby, stood up, took off his coat, put it on his chair and asked if I would look after it whilst he went to the bathroom. He took the dog lead with him.

When he came back he thanked me and asked if he could sit at my table till the people he was waiting for arrived. I told him he could.

"Normally I am a happy man," he said, "but today is not happy for me. I have just shot my dog."

"Why?" I asked.

"Because my girl friend told me she was finished with me. I loved my dog but also I loved her so much I did not think I could live without her. So I took my dog into the woods and shot him with my shotgun, but when I started to raise the gun to my own head I realised my arms were too short and I could not reach the trigger.

"As I wondered what to do a bird started to sing and I changed my mind, because it sounded so full of happiness it gave me hope. But alas I have no dog."

I looked at the lead, which he had placed on top of his coat. "Where is your gun now?"

"I had an urgent need to speak to my girl-friend so I went home and telephoned her.

She agreed to meet me here with a girl friend of hers who is to act as an—how do you say it?—intermediary. They should be here at any moment."

I decided to wait for Dick and the others in the lobby. The man with no dog shook hands and as I left the room two girls entered. They went over to him and one picked up the lead and started to cry.

Dick was coming up the steps; since we had first met he had evolved into a heavy man with the jowls of a St. Bernard. I hoped I wasn't going to go through a period when I would be obsessed by thoughts of dogs.

"You look pretty solemn," Dick said.

"I've just undergone a strange encounter." Bob and John the cameraman joined us, and I told them the story.

"Was the girl pretty?"

"I don't know, John. She might have looked to my dog-bereft friend like Helen of Troy, but she looked quite ordinary to me."

"I can't imagine how anyone would want to kill himself over a woman." Dick shook his head.

I thought of Bea and how badly she had misread him.

We went back to the bar just as the man and two women were coming out. His girl friend had her hand firmly under his arm, but he had the expression of someone who would never be sure of anything again.

CHAPTER EIGHTEEN

Henry Ford claimed that: "History is bunk!" He was famous for some things and infamous for others. When it came to his invention of the endless belt which was the key to mass production, both perceptions applied, and Charles Chaplin starred in a film called *Modern Times* which was a portrayal of the working life of a mass production worker almost too searing to be classified as satire.

In spite of his comment about history, Ford made plenty of it, weaving it as a spider weaves a web, until he died at the age of eighty-three in 1947. One of his major epitaphs could have been that, although a production line was hell, by its very nature it brought heaven. The production line brought down the price of a car until the people assembling it could actually afford one.

By the 1920s the workers at Dearborn could drive out into the countryside in their simple, reliable Model T jalopies and give their children a chance to learn what a fox looked like *in situ.*

Ford relished perversity; he disapproved of the new foundry his son Edsel was building at vast expense and waited patiently till it was completed, whereupon he had it blown up. Edsel died quite young from neuroses brought on by frustration.

When Ford wanted to show everyone who was boss, he turned to a rogue ex-boxer called Harry Bennett and put him in charge of the factory's administration. Bennett agreed to let the Mafia have Dearborn's vegetable concession, thus inviting the mob to help itself to an enormously profitable income.

Ford was a monster who made good and evil almost inextricable, but then perhaps they always are.

An English motor manufacturer who was the complete opposite of Ford in philosophy and practice was Walter Owen Bentley, usually referred to as W.O. I didn't make his acquaintance till he was in his late seventies—he died in 1971. He was an engineer's engineer, quiet and inclined to be conservative; he had a love of quality and did not regard perfection as unattainable. He never ceased trying to excel it.

Ford's primary aim at the beginning of the twentieth century was in due course to put a car in every garage; Bentley immediately after the Armistice twenty years later, wanted to put his cars into only a few garages. These cars were to be for the caviar market, a completely different one from that of Henry Ford; they were owned and driven by young men strong enough to handle huge Bentley sports cars weighing a couple of tons or so, which would wind their way up to a top speed of more than 100 mph at a time when most cars couldn't do much over 40.

Bentleys would be as far above the normal price range as their speed was beyond the average, and their glamorous drivers, who became known as 'The Bentley Boys', were almost as thirsty as the cars.

During the 1920s they partied with a glass of champagne in one hand and a steering-wheel in the other, believing that after the Great War there were no more deaths to be died.

First the War had to be fought, and improving air power was a vital need by the time 1915 was a few months old. As the Western Front started to turn the placid green fields of France and Belgium into the ugly exploding pustules of trench warfare, reliable aerial observation grew increasingly urgent. The Germans, like the French *Communards* a century and a quarter previously during the The Reign of Terror, turned to military observation balloons, as well as to reconnaissance aircraft whose early models were strongly related to their forebears of a few years before. These were dangerously

103

underpowered primitives which lurched across the skies above the trenches and coughed and spluttered like grouse with pneumonia.

Fighter aircraft also were evolving from virtually impotent gliders whose pilots took potshots at each other with pistols, to serious machines of war. Bentley started to modify a French aero engine, the Gnome Rhône Rotary, in which the cylinders went round the crankshaft instead of the more customary operation of crankshaft operating the pistons in the clinders. He teamed up with an aircraft designer and manufacturer called Tom Sopwith, to supply Bentley Rotary engines for both the Sopwith Pup fighter and the far better known Sopwith Camel, often regarded as the best British fighter of the War.

The Bentley was well engineered and unusually used aluminium, which was light enough to give extra speed and reliability, instead of the more usual steel. This diminished the vulnerability of the Sopwiths in combat.

Bentley Motors produced its first car soon after the Armistice was declared in 1918. W.O. claimed that one of the earliest members of the public to hear its maiden bellow as it came down the ramp from the showroom into the street was a hospital sister, who complained about the noise.

"There are people dying in that building!" She pointed at the hospital behind her.

"What a marvellous sound to go out to," W.O. is said to have replied. The sound of a Bentley was unique, and ARGO Records even made and marketed an LP of Bentley engines going through the gears.

My opportunity to meet Bentley occurred when the Automobile Association decided, in the early sixties, to publish a members' magazine called *DRIVE*. I suggested to the editor, Peter Jackson, that I write a piece about the creator of Bentley Motors and he agreed.

"But don't just do an interview with him; he deserves more than that. After all, he's a man whose cars won Le Mans five times in seven years and symbolised an era, apart from all the other extraordinary things he's done, racing motor-cycles and creating marine and aero engines.

"I know—why don't you take him down to Filton to have a look at Concorde under construction?"

"Damn good idea."

"We could really make a day of it for him. We'll lay on a chauffeur-driven car, something fast and rare. How about a Jensen FF?" This was the first four-wheel drive sports saloon.

I was enthusiastic, and Peter's secretary set about making arrangements.

Bentley and his wife Margaret lived in a cottage in Shamley Green, a village just outside Guildford; the car in his driveway was a Morris 1000. I felt almost ashamed to arrive in a chauffeur-driven four-wheel drive Jensen FF to take him to London, but the chauffeur put his foot down hard as soon as we turned into the main road, and W.O. was obviously entranced as the speedometer needle swung effortlessly past the 100 mph calibration.

"Good Lord, we're already going faster than my Le Mans cars along the Mulsanne Straight!" The atavistic ecstasy of the race track was obviously still strong in him.

It was the Bentley Boys who had first generated this enthusiasm and newsreel film of the day shows them—Woolf 'Babe' Barnato, South African heir to the Kimberley diamond mine fortune, Sir Henry 'Tim' Birkin, Dr. J. Dudley Benjafield and others—in the pits at Le Mans or racing high up on the banking at Brooklands, their huge cars dangerously close to the rim of the track.

The Bentley Boys were a vital part of the Bentley mystique, and the Bentley mystique was composed of such factors as the personalities of the cars, their raucous superiority, and the society aspect which gave the impression that they raced through a land of dreams rather than having any contact with the harsh facts of commerce.

That harshness overwhelmed Bentley with the Great Crash of 1929, which W.O. blamed for the marque's passing. As he was a brilliant engineer but not in any respect a money man or manager, the company would almost certainly have gone bust anyway. At least it had been rescued by Rolls Royce, on one terrible condition: the contract with Bentley stipulated that although W.O. could design and build cars or contribute to their construction, he could not 'sign' them. The work he did for Lagonda and Napier, for example, had to be anonymous.

After we had boarded the train at Paddington, Bentley's presence was honoured with an announcement through the newly-installed intercom: "We are happy today to welcome aboard the great railway engineer Mr. Walter Owen Bentley." After that we were invited to travel in the cab of a new Diesel, and W.O enjoyed himself discussing Victorian steam locomotives and railways with the driver until we arrived at the Bristol Factory siding at Filton Halt and made a specially scheduled stop. Three new Bristol cars were lined up to take us to the factory nearby, where we were to have lunch before being escorted to the hangar where Concorde was under construction.

"She's going to be as easy to fly as a Tiger Moth," the PRO extolled the aggressively beautiful jet, as we stood below an engine nacelle. "London to New York in just over three hours in absolute comfort, at the speed of a rifle bullet."

W.O. had an answer ready. "Thank God I'm too old to fly," he murmured.

106

Cecil Arthur Lewis, who flew the Sopwith Camels whose rotary engines W.O. Bentley had designed, came to prefer the more stable SE5a fighter. Whereas the Camel was malicious and inclined to turn on its pilot and kill him as a punishment for the slightest mistake, especially on take-off and landing, the SE5a provided a steadier gun platform and was more robust.

When I met Lewis he was ninety-one and still looked like an advertisement for a Guards Regiment, six feet four in height and as straight as a grounded rifle. We had never met previously but I felt as if I knew him well; in 1936 he had published his book *Sagittarius Rising* which I read more than once. It was not only the most informative book about the life of a fighter pilot ever written, but displayed the poetry and courage which illuminated that life.

Lewis left Oundle and gave a false age in order to join the RFC as a pilot; he was helped by his considerable height of well over six feet to convince his examiners that he was seventeen, the minimum age at which he could be officially accepted, rather than the sixteen he actually was.. He showed great aptitude as a pilot, learning to fly in some ninety minutes. Unlike most other pilots undergoing training, Lewis survived the Great War, which mystified him. The only bullet to hit him creased his back but didn't penetrate his body; he had leaned forward just as it was fired to adjust one of his guns, and being an accurate shot the enemy pilot had therefore failed to kill him.

Lewis won an MC for fighting in a Morane Saulnier Parasol above the Somme; becoming a test pilot for Vickers after the War he was seconded to train the Chinese Air Force. "Unfortunately, the Chinese showed no aptitude in the air," he commented, and when the last one had crashed to his death there was no point in trying to train another intake, so he came home.

He became interested in writing for radio and joined 2LO, forerunner of the BBC, on Savoy Hill. When the BBC was given its charter Lewis shared an office with the first Director General, John Reith, and became friendly with a frequent visitor to the Corporation, George Bernard Shaw. Shaw asked Lewis, not long after he became Programme Manager, to broadcast a new Shavian play, which Lewis did.

His reward came when the film producer Gabriel Pascal wanted to make a movie of Shaw's play Pygmalion, and his permission was conditional on the screenplay being written by Cecil Arthur Lewis, who received an Academy Award for it. Later Pygmalion evolved into *My Fair Lady*.

Just before we parted, I asked him what he was working on in Corfu. "I'm learning to fly a microlight." We shook hands and he turned and strode off, personifying the title of one of his books: *Never Look Back*, (which he qualified with the tag line: *An Attempt At Autobiography*.) He was a man who lived many lives, and won many glittering prizes.

So did Sir Oswald Mosley, whom I went to see in 1976, but he threw them all away. He had the intelligence and charisma that could have made him a great man, and the only man in British political life who could equally well have been a Labour, Conservative or Liberal Prime Minister. He was an aristocrat and a plutocrat; what did for him was that he was also a populist. Seldom in the history of England has a born leader so spectacularly derailed himself; instead of heading for Downing Street, he took the track which at the outbreak of the Second World War led to a prison cell and accusations of being a traitor.

In the Great War he had fought both as a pilot in the RFC and in the 16th Lancers; what started him on the way to the cell in which he spent the Second War was his decision in the early 30s to forsake the ways of Parliament in order to wage sad little rabblerousing battles across the East End of London. He marched at the head of his street army of roughs and toughs, the Blackshirts, through the Jewish and Communist near-ghettos of Stepney and Shoreditch, taunting and provoking their inhabitants. By any standards that was a menacing but tawdry and petty objective, irrelevant to any credible ambition.

When Mosley published a letter in The Times in 1972 about the poor quality of contemporary MPs and their speeches so lacking in wit and felicity of phrase, I wrote to him asking for an interview. As a consequence I received an invitation to visit him at his home, Le Temple de Gloire, beside the Seine at Orsay, about sixty kilometres outside Paris, which had once belonged to another populist, namely Napoleon.

The house was imposing but not vast. Mosley was built on similar lines to his RFC compatriot Cecil Lewis, tall and ramrod straight. He led me into the dining-room, which had as its centrepiece a table which could also have belonged to Napoleon, its deep, mellow patina reflecting the room's gentle light. The table had a minimalist aspect, supporting only a bottle of Johnny Walker Black Label and two heavy and capacious crystal whisky tumblers.

Mosley filled one and skated it across the table to me before pouring a second glass. Although I am Jewish myself, I bore Mosley no rancour, perhaps because I felt the poison had been siphoned out of him with the years, and he still had immense charm.

I asked him about his first wedding—he had married twice. His bride was Cynthia Curzon, daughter of Lord Curzon, at one time Viceroy of India and also Foreign Secretary.

"King George and Queen Mary were guests, weren't they?" I asked.

"Yes, they were there. And the King and Queen of the Belgians. The reason they were there was because they were good friends of my father-in-law, who was Foreign Secretary at the time. He had them staying in his house during the War, so they were intimate friends of his, as were our own King and Queen."

I asked him if, after his experiences during the War, he felt any diffidence about marrying into the higher reaches of the aristocracy.

"No. You see, we all came from the same old country stock and Curzon was originally the same sort of person. But with his enormous talents he lifted himself up to be a Leader of the House of Lords and a marquis and all the rest of it. But we all began more or less in the same place.

"Curzon always said to me—when I was going into the Labour Party—'I don't mind what you do as long as you don't become an isolated individual like Hugh Cecil'. The great thing is not to be a dilettante, but to be serious in politics, and be joined up with a serious force of some kind. It's one of the essentials of being a successful politician to have a good power base. Curzon was very broad-minded despite his rigid Conservative convictions."

The bottle skated between us again. I decided I had got into the rhythm of things, and was not in danger of losing control, but my voice on the tape afterwards indicated that I had developed an exaggerated drawl. But then so had Mosley.

"Sir Oswald, what made you join the Labour Party after being a Conservative MP? Was it simply a form of rebellion?"

Mosley's eyes flared with an old fire. "It was a passionate desire to get something done for the mass of the people. You see, we had all come back from the War with every sort of promise from Lloyd George and the others." He was not only reliving the rage of all those years ago but also clinging on to the slightest justification to have behaved as he did subsequently. "Lloyd George was a very brilliant man," he went on, "but he wasn't allowed to do even one of the things he had promised."

110

We had a top-up each; Mosley's face was still handsome and animated under the wens and blotches of old age. It was difficult to imagine a man of such stature and dignity throwing a brick through someone's window to make a political point.

"There were a hundred and fifty young ex-servicemen in the first Parliament after the War—I was Secretary of their organisation. When it turned out to be impossible to do anything for them through the Conservative Party, the natural thing was to go independent. I won two elections as an Independent, and went on to the Labour Party, which represented the mass of the people and was determined to do something for them. It was not until they completely betrayed everything they stood for at that time that I moved on, in the final gesture of despair if you like, into the Fascist movement. I wanted to get something real done in the world, and of course the Fascist movement in England was a totally different movement from that in Germany or Italy."

"But your movement had very close ties with their Fascist movements."

"Well, the so-called ties were these: in each country, the ex-servicemen after the War, having been betrayed by the breaking of every pledge, decided to start ultra-national movements."

He went on to develop the *lebensraum* theme of the Germans wishing to expand their territory sufficiently to have the space to unite their fellow Germans in the East of Europe. He, on the other hand, had wanted to develop the British Commonwealth and nation to the benefit of all the races within it. He was definitely trying to excuse himself; what I was listening to was about to crumble into an apologia for brutality in Cable Street.

"I couldn't have been a racialist [sic] even I'd wanted to, which I didn't. If I'd been a racialist, I should have blown the British Empire to pieces, as it was composed of every race under the sun."

I could feel myself getting impatient with him. "It's difficult to believe that a man of your intellect would have countenanced the sort of activity that took place in the East End in those days," I said.

Mosley's speech pattern was becoming brittle and distorted; claiming that his fascist Blackshirts were absolutely forbidden to attack individuals or property among their opponents, he went on when I taxed him with anti-Semitism: "When I was in the quarrel with certain Jews—not all Jews, but with some Jews—they would join up and take cover in what they called political action, which it wasn't at all. It was simply venting old dislikes. 'Never attack a man for what he is, only for what he does', was my motto at the time."

That sounded less like sweet reason than an exhausted cliché, and I wondered what he meant by using the past tense relative to 'motto': was he after all advocating a change to violence against a man for what he was?

"You can sit in an ivory tower churning out ideas which, if you're lucky, will be accepted two or three generations afterwards," he went on, "that's being a man of thought." His tone was accusing. "Now I was also a man of action. That's when the trouble begins, because some people oppose you, fiercely and violently. So you *have* to become a demi-god in order to persuade the mass of the people." He stared at me intently, as if he was indeed an avatar, conjured out of space and arrived to perch among the merely mortal, to give leadership and guidance. He was a man who believed in his own godhead; his voice took on an almost litanical cadence.

"I came out of the study and into the field," he proclaimed, "and held the largest public meetings ever held in Great Britain. I wanted to save the British people from themselves, because they were becoming decadent!"

The demi-God sent the bottle skidding towards me once more, as if to confirm that there were no ill feelings between us. However,

112

Mosley's view of the British people seemed to have suffered a sea change; instead of being the victims of broken promises on the part of every war leader, they were now decadent and needed Mosley, like some sort of department store Jesus, to play Saviour. It seemed to me that the words in Mosley's mouth were not so much his as Hitler's; one of the late Führer's final orders, to flood the Berlin underground and drown a sizable portion of the population, was given on the grounds not only of tactics to try to hold up the Russians but because 'the German people are not worthy of me!' I decided to press Mosley on his relations with Hitler.

Mosley answered: "I met Hitler twice, in '35 and '36, and had two conversations: whether it was necessary for Germany and Britain to fight each other and cause a third world war. I did not want another war and we came to the conclusion it was not necessary because we wanted completely different things.

"As I said to you earlier on, Hitler wanted to unite the Germans in Eastern Europe whereas I wanted to continue and develop the British Empire.

"We arrived at a Concordat, and had I been head of the British Government when Hitler attacked Poland, I would not have intervened."

It seemed to me very fortunate for the Poles that Mosley had failed to be elected Prime Minister; although their suffering had been extreme at least it hadn't been officially sanctioned by the British Government. I changed the subject to something else which intrigued me.

"Is it true that you invited Hitler to your second wedding, Sir Oswald?"

"Well, yes, he was certainly there," he answered defensively, "and I'll tell you why. I had my future wife living in the country (England) and I was threatened every day with murder. She could have been

113

attacked herself at any time unless I defended her with a large force of Blackshirts. Therefore I arranged to have the wedding in Germany. So Hitler by invitation from Frau Goebbels, who was a friend of his and of my wife, said that he would be present." He added: "And I thought that too was in the interests of peace."

I probably looked as sceptical as I felt: I was being treated to a show of raw megalomania. Not many people were infected with it, but those who were had dramatically reduced the number of the world's population. It was, I thought, likely that Mosley would have claimed his share of victims, given the chance. He continued on the defensive: "You've got to be friendly with these people if you want peace."

He seemed to have forgotten that his principal wedding guest had died in a rat-hole with a suicide's bullet in his deranged brain as a post-mortem gallon of flaming petrol consumed him. He had also forgotten—or rashly ignored—his first father-in-law's advice never to be in isolation without a power base.

CHAPTER NINETEEN

Bea Francis rang me one Sunday lunchtime and asked me if I could bring down a bottle of tonic water. I happened to be with a girl friend called Denise, who was tall and had a weak back and a Roman Catholic conscience. It was her habit on Sundays to go to Mass and put our relationship on her list of sins for confession. After that, in exchange for a minor penance she received absolution and came back to the flat to initiate the following week's sins with breakfast in bed.

Bea opened her door and I handed her the tonic water.

"Will you join me in a g & t, Walter?"

"That's kind of you Bea, but I'm not alone. Where's Dick?"

"Where do you think? At a meeting. It's quite serious, actually. Someone high up at the BBC discovered Dick's name on the list of applicants for a licence for Yorkshire TV."

"I didn't know he'd planned to do that."

"Neither did I. He could lose his job."

"That would be rather small-minded of the Corporation, wouldn't it?"

Bea shrugged and sipped her drink. "Dick doesn't realise how many people he brushes the wrong way."

"Rubs up," I corrected her. "Forgive me, your English is very good— "

"No, I asked you always to correct me—thank you so much for the tonic."

"My pleasure, Bea." I kissed her cheek and went back upstairs. Denise was in stasis mode. "My back aches," she said. "I think it's my vertebrae—they're not strong enough to cope with my height." I

115

found her strangely attractive, even though she suffered from a down-turned mouth which unavoidably gave her the expression of a martyr dodging an arrow on her way to Beatitude. At least she didn't claim the pain in her back was a negative reward from God for having an affair.

Salvation, as it turned out, was waiting in the wings: Denise's back was to be cured by an osteopath called Stephen Ward.

We met in a nightclub called The Paintbox, in Foley Street, one of the narrow thoroughfares in the neighbourhood of Broadcasting House, the Portland Place headquarters of the BBC. The club was run by a diminutive model called Adele de Havilland, who was under five feet tall. She compensated for her lack of height with a strong personality and dangerously high stiletto heels, combined with a hairstyle known as a beehive, which was nearly as tall as she was and has been exemplified for years on television by Marge Simpson's.

The Paintbox's speciality was a minute semi-circular stage with curtains and two or three easels placed round it, so that customers so inclined could sketch or paint the nude who posed centre stage. Under the Lord Chamberlain's rules of the day, anyone on stage naked was, under the full power of the law, forbidden to move. If a wasp settled on a model's nipple she had to put up with it even if it stung her; to brush it away was to incur the possibility of jail.

Adele greeted us and brought over my drink. "See that chap over at the easel? That's Stephen Ward, the Society osteopath. He's the only artist ever to be given permission to sketch MPs from the floor of the House of Commons: the Prime Minister gave it himself."

"Is he Stephen Ward's patient?" I asked.

"Everybody in Society's Stephen's patient—the Prime Minister, Douglas Fairbanks, David Astor, God knows how many of the members of the peerage—"

"I didn't know so many people had bad backs, Adele."

116

"Well the way they carry on, like a field full of bunnies with titles, you can't be really surprised, can you?"

I think Denise's back had started to trouble her after she and I met. I had heard of Stephen Ward, who had the reputation of being an osteopath, an excellent artist in crayons, and something of a social climber; not necessarily a good idea when Society was rapidly descending.

"Would you like to meet Stephen?" asked Adele, as he got up from his seat at the easel and picked up the drawing.

"Yes please." Adele beckoned him over, a dapper man with glasses and plenty of glossy hair. He showed us his drawing of the model, executed with style and panache.

"Please sit down, Doctor Ward."

"Thank you. Do call me Stephen."

"Stephen. Denise, Walter. What would you like to drink?"

"May I have a negroni?"

"Of course." I wasn't sure what a negroni was, but have had my share since I found out that night in 1960.

"I saw your sketches in the Telegraph, Stephen. I thought they were impressive. What a bastard Eichman was. I'm damn glad the Israelis got him," said Denise.

"He was a pretty chilling creature."

Eichman, a notorious Nazi killer and railway bureaucrat had had the job of making sure that the trains carrying Jews to their deaths in concentration camps ran on time; in spite of Germany simultaneously waging war on two fronts he had efficiently allocated the trains and routes and had also been happy to kill some victims with his own hands.

Using a Nazi escape route set up after the war to enable some of the more wanted war criminals to escape to South America, Eichman fled to Argentina. It had taken the Israeli Nazi-hunters some fifteen years to find and kidnap him and bring him to Israel for trial.

Stephen Ward had been commissioned by the Daily Telegraph to be its court artist in Jerusalem during the trial, and as a result many influential doors were opened to him on his return home. Invitations to various social functions jostled like homing pigeons on the mantelpiece of his Devonshire Street consulting rooms, and Lord Astor leased a cottage to him in the grounds of his sumptuous estate at Cliveden.

Not long after meeting Stephen at the Paintbox I took Denise to see him professionally, with the result that he put her on a course of treatment which cured her back, and charged only a nominal fee. "I know it's said there's no such thing as friendship in business, but that's balls. Of course there's friendship in business—isn't that one of the ways in which you make friends in the first place? It's certainly helped me. It's called recommendation," Stephen said, when I commented on his generosity.

A few weeks later I was able to reciprocate when Brian Inglis, a distinguished journalist and presenter of the weekly TV show *All Our Yesterdays,* asked me if I knew an osteopath. He had just finished a new book on homoeopathic medicine and needed an osteopath to check the relevant chapters

"I do know one as a matter of fact. Chap called Stephen Ward. He cured my girl-friend's back which used to 'freeze' and he's invited me to go with him to a *'vernissage'* at the Leggatt Brothers art gallery in Jermyn Street next week to celebrate his saving Hugh Leggatt's life. Leggatt fell off a horse and broke his neck and every orthodox quack said he'd never walk again, but Stephen proved them wrong."

"Fine, I've read about him. If he's amenable to acting as an editor bring him along for a bite of lunch and I'll let him have the manuscript."

I remember Brian cooked a fluffy omelette which we washed down with burgundy, after which Stephen took the manuscript back to his consulting rooms. I went with him part of the way, and we stopped at a coffee shop in Marylebone High Street.

We had just sat down and ordered when a beautifully tailored black man came in with a companion. "He's one of my dearest friends!" exclaimed Stephen, leaping to his feet. He seized the man's hand and chatted to him; the man's expression grew increasingly bewildered.

"Charming fellow," Stephen said, when he finally sat down again."High Commissioner for Upper Volta."

It was the first sign I had that there was something strange about Stephen, that he could on occasion give way to fantasy, and that fantasy could get the upper hand.

He was also capable of eccentricity; one evening his dishevelled white Jaguar XK 120 drew up alongside me as I was about to go into my local, the King's Head in Forset Street. The car's fuel cap was stuck down with a piece of pink Elastoplast as usual, and the paintwork was leprous and sprinkled with rust. A beautiful young platinum blonde I had seen Stephen with on several occasions was sitting in the passenger seat, sealed into a silk silver lamé evening dress. Stephen was wearing a dinner jacket. As always he looked dapper and smoothly groomed, except that as he climbed out of the car I saw that he was holding up his trousers.

"Can you by any chance lend me a pair of braces, dear boy?" he asked me. "We're on our way to John Paul Getty's house-warming at Sutton Place, and mine came apart as I was putting them on. I can't buy another pair in time because the shops won't be open again till tomorrow."

"I don't wear braces myself, but I can ask the landlord here if he'll lend me some for you."

"That would be kind. I'd make the wrong sort of impression if my trousers fell down." Henry the landlord was dour but agreed to help out. "I wouldn't lend anyone my best pair, but he's welcome to my second best ones." I bore the braces out to Stephen in a triumph they didn't really deserve, being bilious green and frayed.

"Bless you, Walter, you've saved the day, or rather the evening. Would you mind doing them up at the back—I can't quite get them round the buttons." I managed to fasten them whilst he did a sort of fossilised arabesque, and watched him climb back into the car.

"Have a good time," I wished them, "and remember, if you want to use the phone at Getty's, according to the papers, you'll be charged for the call."

Stephen laughed. "I suppose if you're one of the richest men in the world, you're entitled to make a hobby of being mean. Anyhow, I don't anticipate making any calls."

"Well make sure you've got change." He watched the girl open her evening bag and produce a small silk purse, which she opened to show some coins. He waved and the grubby, beautiful little car burbled round the corner into the Edgware Road.

CHAPTER TWENTY

I was allowed to bring a tape recorder to Stephen's private viewing at the Leggatt Brothers Gallery. The guests there who had sat for Stephen were mostly peers, cabinet ministers, and MPs, including Duncan Sandys, Churchill's son-in-law and Secretary of State for Commonwealth Relations.

The exotic Nubar Gulbenkian was also a guest. Gulbenkian was a multimillionaire whose father Calouste had earned his money and his nickname 'Mr. Five Per Cent' through a series of deals he had negotiated between the oil and gas companies exploiting the North African and Middle Eastern fields and the countries which owned them.

He eventually set up The Gulbenkian Foundation in Lisbon, whilst Nubar became one of the principal social ornaments of the London scene. He, like the Duke of Edinburgh, travelled round London in a specially designed and built taxi, whose roof was high enough for him to enter the vehicle wearing a top hat. Every day, his buttonhole was graced by a fresh orchid. Sandys, not known for being demonstrative, gave Stephen a hug when we arrived, and Lord Shawcross, a Labour peer who had been Counsel for the Prosecution at the War Crimes trials at Nuremberg, joked that he had no idea which way up a modern work of art should be hung, and in matters artistic—and only matters artistic—was conservative.

Gulbenkian came up to Stephen to utter praises of the way he thought he had been represented: "Speaking of the exhibition as a whole I thought the three Gs were best: Gulbenkian, Getty, and Gaitskell," he concluded.

John Paul Getty, apart from his payphone in the hall of Sutton Place, was notorious for being one of the richest men in the world and at the same time refusing to pay a ransom of $17 million demanded by the kidnappers of his grandson when, at the age of sixteen, he was snatched in Rome.

It was only when the boy's ear, cut off with a razor, was sent to Getty after five months of argument that he finally paid a ransom of just over two million dollars. His grandson was released, but the boy was permanently damaged by the experience and the drugs he took, finally overdosing on heroin which put him, paralysed and almost blinded, in a wheelchair for the next thirty-five years or so, when he finally died.

Stephen, without seeking to be particularly provocative, sometimes referred to Getty as 'a sweet man'. The middle Getty, his son, was a philanthropist and altruist, and to those who thought of conscience in religious terms, did his utmost through kindness and generosity to be his father's redeemer.

Lord Boothby was also at the *vernissage*. Boothby was a popular Conservative MP before becoming a peer, but was revealed after his death in 1986 to have committed perjury, sodomy—with the rent boys he shared with the leading London gangster Ron Kray, one of the Kray Brothers—and adultery, with Lady Dorothy Macmillan, the Prime Minister's wife. He had a plangent voice suited to infusing the blackest lies with a note of conviction, and his perjury had fraudulently earned him £40000 from *The Sunday Mirror Newspaper*, after swearing in a letter to *The Times* that he was completely innocent of the Mirror's charges, and outfacing the Court. Only after his death were his sins found out and restitution made.

Another of Stephen's connections, a girl called Christine Keeler, was the girl friend of a West Indian jazz singer, Aloysius 'Lucky' Gordon—a nickname which, it turned out, was a serious misnomer.

He underwent an attack of extreme jealousy and fired a bullet at Christine. He missed her and hit the Macmillan Government instead, precipitating what was to become known as the Profumo Affair, which wrecked Profumo's career and brought about Stephen Ward's ruin and suicide.

Blatantly persecuted by the new Home Secretary, Henry Brooke, and accused of living off immoral earnings, plotting espionage on behalf of the Soviet Union, and anything else Brooke could throw at him, Stephen Ward found himself flung into social quarantine by the 'friends' he so valued.

His consulting room shelves, once so crowded with invitations, became permanently empty. Telephones used to issuing paeans of praise, became silent. Backs were turned on him and the greetings and embraces he was used to from the great, good and famous, were exchanged for expressions carrying no recognition. The pace of Stephen Ward's march into fantasyland increased.

He was acting, he claimed, as liaison between Prime Minister Harold Macmillan, the Soviet Secretary of the Communist Party Nikita Kruschev, and President Kennedy, in order to avoid atomic war.

As the days passed it was obvious that Stephen was in danger of imminent arrest. He, Brian Inglis and I had lunch together for what turned out to be the last time. "Stephen, I can offer you any organ of communication—the Sunday Times, Sunday Dispatch, the BBC, ITV, anything to put your point of view." Brian was emphatic. "You *must* make your case against the accusations that have been made against you, take advantage of anything in order to put your point of view. WHAT—REALLY—HAPPENED?"

Stephen chuckled. "Of course, England is a brothel and Macmillan is the Madame." Brian and I looked at each other in despair; even now, Damocles didn't seem to realise that the sword was about to drop. Three days after our lunch Stephen was arrested and charged with 'living on immoral earnings' and conspiracy to commit espionage. Six weeks after his arrest he took an overdose of sleeping pills and died.

My recording of the Leggatt Brothers' party for Stephen got mislaid for some thirty years before I discovered it in the back of a wardrobe. It contains the only example of Stephen's voice discussing the art of sketching and his personal take on it. His tone is heavy with charm and there is no suspicion that the people queuing up to praise him are not really friends at all, but shadows.

CHAPTER TWENTY-ONE

W Somerset Maugham stood in his suite at The Dorchester in the posture of shrivelled old age. A long pendulum of mucus dangled from his nose, to be hastily wiped off by his long-time catamite secretary, Alan Searle. Maugham was precisely and handsomely dressed in a check suit, but there was little for it to mould itself to. The renowned author looked as if in need of food, much as he had described himself in an early novel, starving to death as a medical student in nineteenth century London.

Yet Maugham possessed a sort of off-beat charm, a still potent personality, the presence of legend. He had published some of the best-known books and plays ever written, and I had read or seen a good many of them. He often wrote from a remote and cynical focus, ruthlessly examining human frailty through a magnifying glass.

When I tried to interview him, I soon realised I was too late. He stuttered a few sentences, but absolute coherence was beyond him. For some reason I cannot remember, I asked him about his contemporary Rudyard Kipling, an author I greatly admired. When I mentioned *Stalky & Co,* the somewhat cruel novel based on Kipling's Victorian schooldays at a school at Westward Ho! in Devon, Maugham exclaimed: "Horror! Horror! Horror!"

There wasn't really enough to broadcast, but as it was Maugham Betty Rowley, the large and formidable editor of the *Today Programme* at the time, would probably have used it. However, she wanted me to edit out Maugham's stutter, which I refused to do, as it was natural to him and not simply the result of old age.

ARGO Records gave a party at Johnny Koon's Lotus House to celebrate the launch of *Theatre 60* at the beginning of 1961. Harley

Usill and Dick Francis had edited my interviews so that the result sounded as if the protagonists were gathered round a table to articulate their views on the theatre.

The final cast consisted of Dame Sybil Thorndike and Siobhán McKenna; Noël Coward, Peter Ustinov, and Peter Hall, who in due course became theatrical knights, and Harold Pinter and Albert Finney, who were offered knighthoods and turned them down. Pinter eventually soared into the stratosphere of honours when in 2005 he won the Nobel Prize for Literature, although he failed to show up on the podium and accepted the prize by pre-recorded videolink.

For this lack of graciousness he received 1.3 million dollars, the award of which was not unanimously welcomed, especially by traditionalists who believed that speech should consist of words, not largely of pauses, the hallmark of Pinteresque dialogue. Another hallmark was its spikiness, as if the roles of his leads were designed to be played by cacti.

Sean Kenny died young of alcoholism, which produced a cerebral haemorrhage and heart attack. He managed to make his mark on the theatre even so, inventing stages which did away with proscenium arches and became an integral part of the play. Sean was responsible for the stage design of some forty productions, and also won several Tonys. He was only forty-three when he died, a man whose Muses could not overcome his Furies.

Kenneth Tynan's stutter did not get in the way of his clarity of thinking and the determination of a crusader. He was influential in doing away with the Lord Chamberlain's office and helping to bring *Oh Calcutta!* to the stage—the first time a nude revue had been thus presented. Another first was Tynan's use of the word 'fuck' on the BBC.

When Laurence Olivier became the first Director of The National Theatre, which Tynan had been clamouring for for years, he became its literary and publicity manager for ten years, from 1963-73, although he died quite young and his voice these days is barely an echo beyond a distant horizon.

The Thames still rustles past the formidably ugly building which so solidly contradicts the ephemerality of the stage which Tynan loved and revered so much, and round its granite profile swirl the spirits of all the egos he wounded in his battles and rebellions against authority.

He could be endearing, but didn't often bother.

CHAPTER TWENTY-TWO

In 1965, a young Italian-American called Bob Guccione started a new magazine for men in London called Penthouse. Rather in the style of the author Renè Balzac in the 1880s, Bob was under siege from his creditors; whereas Balzac rose before dawn to write his way out of trouble with novels such as *Eugenie Grandet*, which did very well, Bob had to use his ingenuity to distribute his new publication without the help of W.H. Smith, whose chairman he was reputed to have greatly offended with the first mock-up of *Penthouse.*

W.H. Smith was a Quaker company, and to be a Quaker was to be equated with being a Puritan. The story was that when the chairman's secretary found herself staring down at pages of nude girls photographed from many intimate angles, she shrieked, and Penthouse was remorselessly banned from Smith's as a weapon of the Devil.

Taking a less condemnatory attitude, a magazine called *New English Library* was persuaded to share its distribution outlets with Penthouse and so saved the new magazine's day.

Bob Guccione's early aim was to ensure that Penthouse would be a quality publication. He himself was a skilled cartoonist and photographer, and always encouraged good writing. When I started to write for him, he told me that catching up Hugh Heffner and making Penthouse more successful than *Playboy* was a priority.

Because of W H Smith's embargo, finding advertisers to contribute to Penthouse was almost impossible, and we contributors were paid very little. Dr Alex Comfort, who was to write *The Joy of Sex* and make a fortune—I think the book sold fourteen million in paperback—was one of my co-writers, and sometimes I would write a short story and publish an article under a pen-name, in the same issue. For a time I also became Penthouse's motoring correspondent, my cardinal rule being to test only cars I couldn't afford.

Another new magazine founded in London in 1965, with the intention of competing with *Playboy*, was *Mayfair*. Sadly its proprietor, Brian Fisk, was accidentally killed when his Mercedes Benz turned over just outside East Grinstead. My personal recollection of him is his pleasure at picking up a gold-handled Victorian umbrella cheaply at a railway Lost Property auction.

Paul Raymond was the third member of the triumvirate of men's magazine proprietors, although he was primarily a man of property. He owned some thirty-two buildings in Soho, the best-known of which were Raymond's Revue Bar and The Windmill Theatre. He also owned the Whitehall Theatre.

His best-known publication was *Men Only*, in which I published an article a month. Paul paid quite well, but I often had to go to his office to receive my fee from him personally, as he did not regard parting with money as a popular pastime, and would allow nobody else, including his accountant who had an office on his premises, to sign a cheque.

Paul had a Rolls Royce and a chauffeur-bodyguard called Charlie, a dapper, slender man who usually had lunch with him at a cheap Italian restaurant near the Paul Raymond Organisation's offices near Archer Street. Paul's back was narrow and his hair very long, so that he rather resembled the Lion in *The Wizard of Oz*. Charles was always well-groomed.

One of Bob's favourite restaurants was also Italian, but not cheap. It was in the heart of Soho and called The Terrazza. So far as I recall there were three or four Terrazzas, all distinguished by tessellated black and white marble floors.

Bob, tall and with the hawkish look of a Sicilian pirate, always wore an open-neck shirt and favoured gold bling. He had the right sort of neck for it. He drove a large American car and had a powerful telepathic sense which enabled him to keep accurate touch with public taste. One day I remember his warning me that a novel I was planning was on the wrong subject. "What the public wants at this time," he told me, "is not a book like yours about a snobbish society woman but on the lines of a male *Lolita*."

I took his advice which was right as usual, with the result that *Clovis*, which came out in 1970, did reasonably well, although the film option taken out on it did not materialise into movie rights, a far stronger commitment to filming it. To my surprise, as it was an intensely English book, it did quite well in America.

In 1965 the BBC took three of my television plays; they were paid for but alas never produced. Dick Francis became Senior Producer of Panorama and he and Beata moved to a new house in West London, at Roehampton, so that I saw very little of him.

As punishment for what the Corporation regarded as misdemeanours he was in due course sentenced by the BBC to be its Controller in Northern Ireland, when The Troubles were properly under way and spotlights designed to illuminate IRA attempts to attack the Controller's house had the unfortunate side-effect of also keeping him awake. It was for him an arduous period of side-tracked ambition.

The 1960s were a good time to be a motoring correspondent. The early motorways which began to replace the narrow roads filled with oily smoke spurting from the corroded exhausts of out-of-condition lorries were unrestricted. If your car could reach one hundred mph it could do it legally. Meanwhile, many car companies had more than one Press car, and most would lend one to a motoring correspondent for private use if asked nicely. That stopped when OPEC, the oil producers' club, substantially jacked up the price of oil in 1973 and applied an economic wrecking ball to many of the world's economies.

The most exciting car I remember testing was the 161 mph (maker's claim) Iso Grifo.

At 155 mph, the most I could get out of it on the M1, the car gulped 100.1 litres of fuel between Watford and Silverstone. A trio of Shelby Cobras attained 180 mph whilst using the virtually empty motorway as a practice track for Le Mans and there were rumours that someone doing 90 mph as the Cobras flashed past opened his driving door to get out because he thought he'd stopped, and was badly injured as a result.

Amidst a great deal of ill feeling, and with a Minister of Transport who I don't think even held a driving-licence, the 70 mph restriction was eventually introduced.

As a result The British School of Motoring had to close down its special High Performance Course, which occasionally awarded its badge-holders the special prize of driving a Ferrari 330 GTC belonging to BSM's Chairman, the formidable Denise McCann, and journeys inevitably took much longer, removing most of the purpose of having a motorway in the first place. There was no longer much left of the open road.

CHAPTER TWENTY-THREE

I was thoroughly enjoying my writing and broadcasting career, but decided to increase my income by adding another, more lucrative, job to my work portfolio. I was reminded of how uncertain my finances were by an incident with Shelley Winters, when I took her out to dinner and almost ran out of money. She was wearing sables and I was fumbling for enough cash to pay for the seats in a Tottenham Court Road fleapit after an expensive dinner at a place called The Braganza, the flagship restaurant of the Wheeler's chain.

Two things happened: I found I only had enough money for the cheap seats and an usherette recognised Shelley in spite of her reading glasses and in a state of excitement hustled us into the auditorium without checking the tickets I hadn't got, leaving me with just enough cash for a taxi back to the hotel afterwards.

I didn't want a full-time job and had no desire for salaried employment, because I wanted to remain reasonably independent, so being a salesman on commission seemed a good bet, but what should I sell? Certainly not coffee machines; my memories of Donohue and the exploding Dodge would never disappear altogether.

I decided to answer one of the frequently advertised jobs with a life assurance company. The Man From the Pru, cycling round the highways and byways collecting pennies, didn't arouse much fellow feeling but many of the best life offices were Canadian, and as my affection for Canada ran deep—as it still does—I decided to answer an advertisement for a consultant with Imperial Life of Canada's Staples Inn branch in High Holborn. I rang the number and made an appointment to see the branch manager the following afternoon. On the way to the appointment I walked along Chancery Lane, meditating as to whether there would be a chance of testing a Ferrari borrowed from Les Leston, a retired racing driver and Ferrari dealer who had a car accessories shop nearby in High Holborn.

Pondering my approach to Les, whom I had spoken to once or twice, I entered a building, glanced at the list of companies displayed in the foyer and took a lift to the sixth floor.

A receptionist took me in to see the manager, whose name was Freddy Flack, there was an instant sense of warmth, and after a brief meeting I was hired. It then transpired that I had joined Canada Life by mistake.

It made no difference—I enjoyed my relationship with Freddy and the company for about fifteen years, meshing my life assurance and other activities without too much difficulty and occasionally finding a client among my interviewees. The band leader, composer and clarinettist Mr Acker Bilk, for instance, became a client; I had first met him shortly after he emerged from Somerset, where he had been born in a village called Temple Cloud.

In an early publicity still in which I was invited to take part, Acker is wearing a bowler hat and striped waist coat and posing with his band with their instruments, whilst a model called Josie St Clair, who had introduced us, stands to one side wearing a traditional rustic dress and hat. The Victorian bartender wearing an apron and a soup-strainer moustache is the author.

One of the television plays the BBC paid me for, but never produced, would have starred Acker, who flew me out to Dusseldorf, where he was performing at the Schubertshalle concert hall, to discuss the proposition. After composing *Stranger On The Shore* he would probably not have been affordable anyway, but it was at the time a disappointment for Acker as well as for me.

There were several very funny people connected with the Bilk band as well, of course, as Acker himself. One was another Somerset character, whose name was Zank.

It was Zank's habit each day to park in the station yard at Bristol's Temple Mead main line terminus. Free parking had always been permitted, but one morning an officious member of the station staff approached Zank as he was locking up his car.

"That your car?"

"Why do you want to know?"

"Can't park here."

"I've been parking here for years."

"You can't park here any longer. It's a new regulation. Just been brought in."

Zank put his hand in his pocket and jingled the coins there. "Five shillings make any difference?"

"Wouldn't be surprised if it made a deal of difference." The official stretched out his hand.

"Fuck 'ee then," said Zank, and sauntered off.

Another band leader, Kenny Ball, wanted life assurance but not the bother of discussing it; Acker had recommended me and that was enough. All he wanted to do was give me a cheque.

Reluctantly he spent five minutes or so filling in an application form which he put on the bonnet of his car on top of a newspaper to protect the paintwork, wrote out the cheque and handed it to me, and told his chauffeur to drive off. It was the quickest transaction I ever experienced. However, I found by and large that it was too difficult to present myself as a writer, say, to David Frost and at the same time try to sell him an endowment policy, especially in a rehearsal room with Millicent Martin belting out: "That Was The Week That Was."

Barry Took and Marty Feldman were two other life assurance clients I failed to acquire: I had breakfast with them and tried to interest them in assurance but it required too much dilution of concentration.

Those people who become leaders in the world of entertainment— categorised as 'stars'—barely have the time to twinkle at people who do not share their section of sky. They fashion their own worlds and do their best to inhabit them successfully, but very few can enter from outside, any more than a strange lion can find acceptance in a pride or a lone Meercat seeking companionship find it in a tribe of Meercats if it doesn't smell right.

Another major factor, of course, is money. People such as Formula One drivers own yachts and private aircraft and bear the accolade of 'star', but stardom of any sort requires glamour, as well as money, and glamour is one of those frustrating qualities sufficiently abstract and mysterious to be indefinable and almost irrelevant when it comes to the simple vulgarity of trying to acquire it.

Stars can also be found amongst inanimate objects. Although Concorde was conceived originally simply as a project by Sir Arnold Hall, Head of the Royal Aircraft Establishment at Farnborough, it had star quality as soon as it began to take shape. Most of its passengers loved it, as did its crews who, as often as possible when off duty, used to watch it take off or land from a well-sited pub with a garden over which it came thunderously along the flight path just overhead.

When the BBC and the Design Museum held a design competition three years after Concorde had been withdrawn from service in 2003, Concorde defeated both the E-Type Jaguar and the Spitfire for first place.

I found myself elliptically involved with Concorde in an unusual way shortly after she went into service in 1976. A reader's letter was published in *Private Eye* claiming that an Air France Concorde which caught fire on its way to New York on November 24th 1978 at Paris on its way to New York had caught fire owing to over-heating caused by the failure of a bolt securing four other bolts in the highly sophisticated and specially designed air intake system, which was controlled by computers, and burned through the wing.

As there was a good deal of ill feeling in America about Concorde's high decibel engine noise, and in some quarters a determination to stop her flying any American routes, I had the idea of writing a novel about a group of American protesters sabotaging a Concorde. The letter in *Private Eye* seemed to offer a method of doing this, and I was given a couple of excellent and expensive lunches by British Airway's PR chiefs before they fully appreciated what I had in mind, and took fright.

The word went out that Concorde crews were only to have dealings with me in writing and that the PR people were to be the arbiters of whether what I wrote should be published or censored.

I therefore decided to approach Brian 'Trubby' Trubshaw, Chief Test Pilot of Bristol Aeroplanes and the second test pilot in the world to fly Concorde, after Airbus's André Turcat.

"Silly buggers!" Brian said, when I explained why I was ringing him. "Come down to Filton and we'll have a bite of lunch and discuss how to sabotage her."

Both his invitation and his manner when I came into his office reminded me of the RAF pilots I had known during the Second War; he exuded a sort of youthful joy, as well as the gravitas which so often imbues those who risk their lives on a regular basis.

Concorde, in still life pirouettes, posed gracefully against the walls and on the tables; we had a drink before lunch was served and I

136

told Brian about the letter in *Private Eye* and the sort of book I wanted to write. He picked up his telephone handset and dialled a number.

"I'll have a word with my Chief Engineer, Walter. 'Hello, Lofty, I'm in the novel-writing business today. If you wanted to sabotage Concorde by larking about with the engine air intake system, how many bolts would you have to undo? I see. And would that be a feasible way of doing it?' He listened and nodded.

"Right, Lofty. Thanks." He recradled the handset. "He says four bolts. That would probably precipitate a fire as the engines run so hot anyway."

"I'm very grateful, Trubby."

"That's all right. The world's full of anoraks waiting to catch one out, though probably not in this case, because they don't know enough themselves simply to pretend to being better informed that the person they're trying to criticise.. Now, if you have any trouble with the bureaucrats give either Brian Walpole, who runs the Concorde Flight, a call and say I put you on to him, or his side-kick David Leney."

I thanked him again. I did finish my Concorde book, but it was never published. However, I was compensated: David Leney became a lifelong friend.

CHAPTER TWENTY-FOUR

The sixties was an era when there always seemed to be a wide range of things to think and talk about, new customs and practises to praise or condemn, things to rebel against and traditions to protect.

Furthermore, the sixties were quite different from other decades because certain events conspired to distort life's normal perspectives to a point which seemed to render most of the things that gave shape to life insignificant. Perhaps the most powerful of these was the assassination of President Jack Fitzgerald Kennedy in 1963, followed not long afterwards by that of his brother Bobby.

Flower Power coloured America generally and particularly San Francisco, but the flowers which had glistened with the brightness of a bouquet turned into the sad shades of a wreath when the gunshots barked in Dealy Plaza.

Speculation about what really happened in Dallas has meant that the Kennedy myth has always been able to nurture the Kennedy legend and keep it alive. No alternative to the Warren Commission's Report has ever been sufficiently persuasive to permit general conviction. Yet this summation of the worthy judges of the Supreme Court of what really happened was never fully trusted by the public, and many of its questions were not answered but begged. How could a question without an answer solve a mystery?

That question still remains today, and for some fifty-four years the shadow show of the exterior parade and the alleged events inside the prison in Dallas have told disparate stories: Oswald would have had to be a crack shot to hit Kennedy, reload, and hit him again twice, but he wasn't a crack shot. What was the connection—if any—of the night-club owner Jack Ruby, who drew a pistol and killed Oswald in the police station in front of the Press cameras after he had already been arrested for the murder of the President? For that he was himself sentenced to death in 1964, but the sentence was overturned and Ruby was eventually killed by cancer and not by the electric chair. The world wept copiously at the death of JFK and the world is still not enlightened.

One of the most exciting qualities possessed by the President was that he was a dreamer with the power to implement his dreams, the most dramatic of which was that America should be the first nation to land a man on the moon, but sadly Kennedy was to join the vast list of people who down the ages have a dream of noble dimensions and begin to implement it but die before it can come fully to life.

The architect of a cathedral does not expect to live long enough to worship in it himself, but Schubert presumably expected to finish his Eighth Symphony. Kennedy was brutally prevented from seeing his American man on the moon dream realised, whatever his assassin's motive, but why didn't Schubert finish what became known as the Unfinished Symphony? His premature death was far too obvious an answer; we don't know what caused that death. Was it a purely physical or perhaps emotional reason? What do we know of a Warren Commission of the heart?

The most significant sound of the mid-era of the twentieth century was the Morse code rhythm in F-Sharp of the electronic beep. So far as pressure on the National Air and Space Administration (NASA) was concerned, fulfilment of the Kennedy promise was no doubt stimulated by the highly unwelcome sound of the beep emitted from a Soviet satellite called Sputnik, as it regularly passed overhead on its voyage round the globe.

I had never heard what we call a beep; previously computers used to make an entirely different sound, although the shrill, excited protest of the anti-submarine detector which we called ASDIC came close.

The first computer I ever came into contact with was when I went to live in New York and got a temporary job in the new credit card industry: Diners' Club had offices in The Empire State Building, and in those offices computers stood like clusters of Arnold Schwarzeneggers, whilst a variety of what looked like pulley wheels attached to them went into spasmodic half-turns, clockwise and anti-clockwise.

When the wheels had completed whatever they were doing the computer went into stand-at-attention mode and spat out a mouthful of punched cards whilst whirring some sort of computer anthem.

The first time I heard an actual beep was one evening at a friend's house. We were listening to a newscast from an announcer who sounded alarmed to the point of being in shock.

"The Soviet Union has today launched a space vehicle!" we were told. "American security is under threat!" Everything the announcer said was accompanied by a barrage of exclamation marks, but he was interrupted by the far more sinister sound of the voice of Sputnik.

It was a voice devoid of warmth, a voice that had never experienced love or comfort or kindness, and never would. It was not the voice of triumph at being where it was before the Americans caught up, as they were bound to. It was the voice of nothing animate, but an articulation of profound loneliness, the sound of something locked in the solitary confinement of space. It chilled the soul.

Nowadays life without the beep is unimaginable, just as serenity is largely a delight of the past and can barely be remembered; everything has to be at full volume, whether it be the siren from a passing ambulance or fire truck, or the insane metallic screams within the bellowing confines of a night club or dance hall.

The aural damage we have suffered has left it possible to hear but not to listen, and sound has been subsumed in mere noise. The rocket of our future slowly rises before it is abruptly gone, engulfed by the invisible.

CHAPTER TWENTY-FIVE

I emigrated to Brazil for five years after returning to England to be demobilised from my RAF service, which ended in Egypt. I have written about my RAF experiences and Brazil in another book.

Yet again, 1969 was to offer an unusual personal experience: an invitation from Antonio Olinto, the Brazilian Cultural Attaché in London, to visit Rio's first international film festival.

Antonio's wife Rita was regarded in some quarters as a witch or *feitiçeira*, but she and Antonio, who was also a poet, had become friends of mine during my social visits to the Brazilian Chancellery. It seemed a fine opportunity to record some traditional Brazilian folk music, so I asked Harley Usill if he would be interested in my producing one for ARGO.

"I can let you have a stereo Üher to take with you. They're certainly good enough to use for top quality recording and broadcasting. Have you any artists in mind?"

"I can ask Antonio, and I know there are one or two exceptionally fine amateur choirs which sing in churches."

"All right, go ahead. If you find something that seems to have commercial prospects, bloody Decca will probably try to snatch it. Anyway, good luck."

He handed me the Üher, which was actually small enough to fit into my pocket and reproduce a sound like Wigmore Hall. I arrived at Heathrow and before long was looking at the slender, clean line of the VC 10's wing entering a few wisps of cloud which soon grew denser.

Before jets, piston-engined aircraft such as Argonauts had taken thirty-two hours to heave themselves from London to Rio, or slightly less coming back if there was a tail wind.

A VC 10 took about fifteen hours, with stops at Lisbon or Madrid, the Canary Islands, and the north-east Brazilian city of Receife.

As we approached Rio's mountain backdrop, I was invited to the flight deck for a pilot's eye view of our landing. It had been sixteen years since I had re-emigrated from Rio to Toronto and later New York, but it was Rio and its *alegria*, the epitome of a city of romantic indolence, which I most loved, together with its humour and African sense of rhythm.

The domestic airport of Santos Dumont, built on landfill and named for the early twentieth century Brazilian airship and aeroplane designer, appeared ahead, with the tall concrete Christ on the summit of Corcovado watching ubiquitously over his world. The Christ had never seemed to me particularly benevolent; it seemed to be more on the alert for sins to condemn than for sinners to forgive, but the degree of repentance needed to qualify for forgiveness is not included in books of enlightenment.

We landed at the international airport of Galeão and were driven along the road towards the distant city, the mountains on one side and the sea on the other. A white church shone high against the mountainside, and a pervasive smell of sewage cast an olfactory shadow as it seeped from a cluster of huts built on stilts over the shallow, leprous shore and sewage-speckled sea.

I felt nostalgic, remembering my original arrival in Rio, which I had toured by taxi at night with a Russian fellow-passenger from the converted French cargo ship *Groix* on which we had spent nearly three weeks. His name I recalled was Vladimir Popoff. We were both almost dazed by the orange light which cast its late night glow into

Rio's sky; such signs of nocturnal life had not existed in Britain or most of Europe since the long ago days of peace.

Even though the War had been over for three years I felt an instinctive sense of guilt at the sight of light shining through an uncurtained window, and expected punishment to hurtle from the skies for such carelessness.

I was staying at a hotel called The California in Copacabana, and after my fifteen-hour flight went straight to bed. The bedside phone went off almost immediately.

The voice on the other end of the line was English and had a well-balanced drawl. Having identified himself as John Shakespeare, First Secretary and Minister of Information at the British Embassy, and telling me he had read a newspaper article about visitors to the Festival in which my name was included, he invited me over to his apartment for a drink. His address was in Copacabana near my hotel and a drink seemed a good idea, so I gave up thoughts of going back to bed and went.

For a long time now the diplomats whose antecedents revelled in Rio's beauty and amenities have had to conform with postings to Brazilia, in effect a jungle city created by the iron will of a Brazilian President of Polish ancestry, Juscelino Kubitscheck, who saw it as a way of opening up Brazil's vast interior, and daringly conceived by Oscar Niemeyer, a Brazilian architect of Austrian ancestry. Brazilia displaced Rio de Janeiro as Brazil's capital city, and in spite of the wrath generated among government officials and diplomats by this act of what was conceived as deliberate barbarism, Niemeyer lived to be one hundred and four.

In 1969 Rio was still Brazil's capital, and as a guest of the Brazilian Government and member of the British Delegation to the Film Festival I received a generous supply of meal vouchers which I used to pay for dinner parties in hotels and restaurants. John and his wife Lalage became friends of mine, as did various journalists and musicians I met during the course of the events.

It was John who suggested that I should visit a church in the Borough of Tijuca. "I've heard there's a choir which sings there called the Palestrina, led by a chap whose name is Armando Prazeres. Apparently they're pretty good." I thanked him and took a green, open-sided tram to the seaside borough of Tijuca. Some of Rio's trams had been acquired early in the twentieth century through the purchase of bonds, and were therefore nicknamed *bondes*.

They had the posture of maiden aunts with an utterly prim disregard for streamlining of any sort.

There was a monk standing outside a church who acknowledged that the Coral Palestrina often sang there and as it happened was rehearsing this morning. "If you want to listen to Brazilian folk music as it should be rendered, you will find it over there, in the Church of Nossa Senhora de Tijuca."

I thanked him and went inside, to be greeted by the sort of music casual visitors to Brazil seldom encounter. A small group of men and women and the choirmaster Armando Prazeres sang in a way that contained the cadences of fishing-nets and country markets and cowboys and kings of the sea; the music was rich and deep, with repetitive choruses alive with laughter and sorrow.

The voices surged into the African rhythms of the god Xangô before echoing the Vila Lobos stuttering thud of a small up-country locomotive's pistons as it puffs its way through the fields at the edge of the rain-forest.

Slavery in Brazil had only ended late in the nineteenth century, officially in 1887, and one of the reasons for the strong African element in Brazilian culture, particularly along the country's eastern littoral, was that the Portuguese and French, Brazil's principal colonisers, practised miscegenation. There was no colour bar as such, and it was the native Indian population that suffered most from the newcomers and their acquired diseases, not the more hardy slaves from Natal who were invited into their overseers' beds. One sneeze from a European could wipe out an Indian tribe.

When Armando, who told me he had five sons who were all learning to be musicians, agreed to let me record the Palestrina, I set up ARGO's Üher in the nave. It was a light, highly compact recorder with two separate free-standing microphones.

The choir began to sing again and, as usual, although I am a hopeless dancer, I found excitement and the urge to dance almost irresistible, especially when the music was a samba.

This folk music, however, had nothing of the samba about it; the samba was rhythmic and primitive, but what the choir was singing was atavistic and profound. It sang to the singer more powerfully than the singer sang the song, the words were simple but the emotions they expressed deep-rooted and complex. They sang of bargaining with village market-women for their wares, and of a circus clown sadly making people laugh as he travels through the countryside and performs in small country towns. They sang, too, of Cairi, the God of the Sea, worshipped by fishermen on nights of storm.

When I played the recording to Harley on my return to England he decided to bring the LP out the following year, when we held a launch party aboard a Thames restaurant boat for the Brazilian Ambassador and members of his staff.

It was an excellent party, even though, as Harley had predicted, bloody Decca had buggered up the marketing.

CHAPTER TWENTY-SIX

At the end of the Rio Film Festival, I was given permission by the Indian Department of the Brazilian Government to visit the Xingu Indian reservation in the vast jungle of the Mato Grosso, six times the size of Britain and about twelve hundred miles north west of Rio. I would be looked after by Orlando Villas Boas who, with his brothers Claudio and Leonardo, had taken on the immense task of protecting the Indian tribes of the region from extinction at the hands of the *garimperos*, the murderous diamond hunters who usually carried a sieve in one hand and a rifle in the other.

Of the Indian tribes which warred with each other, the most savage and aggressive had been the Xavantes, who also did not hesitate to kill any white man or stranger they came across. The usual Indian method of killing was the club or bow and arrow; blow-pipes with darts whose tips were dipped in lethal poison was their method of killing monkeys and other tree-dwelling animals and birds which contributed to their diet but were usually far out of reach up a tree.

The traditional way explorers wishing to pacify hostile tribes went about it was to leave presents for them near their villages or places in the jungle in which they congregated; the Xavantes especially had a reputation for refusing to be beguiled by the magic of cheap mirrors or beads and applied their clubs to the skulls of would-be donors anyway.

The Villas Boas brothers successfully managed to persuade many tribes to forget their enmity towards each other and form the population of what became an Indian reservation of eight thousand square miles of territory. They were helped by the inexplicable collapse of the Xavantes into desuetude, perhaps because they were finally overwhelmed by a feeling of timeless isolation in a world they no longer really belonged to.

Almost without warning they lost their culture and their pride, and began to shamble about in villages, developing rapidly into towns, such as Xavantina. They did odd jobs or begged, smoked tobacco that had the consistency of hessian and smelled worse while they waited for their spirit to die altogether. That had begun to occur in the early 60s; the tribes which decided to join the reservation at Xingú carried on embracing their own cultures and slowly bonded, but there were cases of Indian villages on which light aircraft flown by white pilots had dropped gifts to entice the villagers outside, and then treacherously dropped sticks of dynamite on them.

My first view of Xingú was from the windows of an ancient DC3 in the livery of the Brazilian Air Force (Força Aerea Brasileira or FAB) which had landed to pick me up at a small military airfield. Metal seats ran along its sides and its cargo included an anonymous vermillion carcass, a little girl who was sick even before the motors started, and several sacks of coffee.

When I went to present my compliments to the pilot, I saw that most of the instruments had been removed and been replaced by portraits of the saints. The crew consisted of eight officers, including a doctor wearing the badge of Hippocrates.

Slowly we grumbled towards the interior, landing to refuel at Goiania, the capital of the state of Goias and stay the night at a hotel where the food, as usual in Brazil, was delicious and offered suckling pig for supper. There were several girls who lived in the hotel and whose rooms were made homely with family photographs and personal possessions such as dolls, sewing and needlework kits, and bonnets. Giant bullfrogs in the garden boomed a bass counterpoint to the enraptured rustling of hordes of crickets, and in the morning an al fresco breakfast was accompanied by a praying mantis trying to catch a humming-bird which teased it by keeping just out of reach with a frenetic beating of its wings as it plunged its long beak into a hibiscus flower.

We took off shortly before ten a.m, jouncing over the grass runway; the starboard engine backfired loudly as we lifted but decided to pick up tune. I wondered what sort of animals our vermillion carcasses had been, and as they seemed to have had heavily-muscled shoulders, thought they had probably been zebu cattle.

Our next landing was at Xavantina, for further refuelling. An arcade of bougainvillea in front of the radio shack seemed to quiver, and I saw that the flowers were alive with hornets. As I had no wish to be pollinated, I hastened back to the DC3. The motors seemed to respond to the throttles with reasonable calm, and we took off and flew over Xavantina towards our next stop, a new town called Aragarças.

The *garimpeiros* had already tried their luck there; a yellowish sandy scab scarred the banks of the Araguia River, whose confluence with the Garças marked the town's birthplace.

The walls of the public urinals did not meet the floor or the ceiling; privacy evidently didn't count for much and one could hear a wide range of multiple farting from almost as far away as the airfield.

Refuelled once more, we took off and flew over the green jungle clumps of the *selva* until the Xingú coiled tightly back on itself in a sort of anacondan stasis, studded with sandbanks and individual lakes.

There were several buildings below, including one whose mast and antenna indicated that it was the radio shack. As we came in to land twenty or so Indians ran to meet us, shouting requests for cartridges: "Cartouchos! Cartouchos!"

149

A plump, bearded man with long hair and a brilliantly coloured parrot on his shoulder came out of the radio shack and exchanged words with the air force doctor, who gave him a box. He carried it over to the shack and took it inside, afterwards coming over to shake hands.

"I am Orlando Villas Boas," he said. "A signal from our Indian Department in Rio has told me that you are my guest. As I do not know you I cannot give you as warm a welcome as I would wish, but hopefully warmth will establish itself."

"I am sure it will. Do we use first or family names?"

"If all is well we shall use each other's first names eventually so let us be optimistic and use them to start with." He shaded his eyes and the parrot squawked as the DC3's engines roared and it swung round to taxi back down the grass strip on which we had landed. Several Indians carried the meat and sacks of coffee towards a cookhouse and presumably stowed them; an encouraging puff of smoke from the building's tall chimney drifted skyward, spreading a smell of fish.

Orlando was wearing beige shorts and slippers, and over supper— a large river fish eaten by spooning out the flesh behind the gills and continuing to fillet the fish with a spoon —we started talking about Colonel Percy Harrison Fawcett, the English explorer who disappeared in the Mato Grosso jungle in 1925.

"Fawcett made a very bad mistake," said Orlando, "especially here in the jungle. He overlooked his old friends in his efforts to make new ones—in this case, he teased his old friends by frightening them."

"How did he do that?"

"He took out his false teeth and pretended he was eating with them by opening and closing the jaws. The Indians had never seen or heard of false teeth. They were terrified.

"So as Fawcett was climbing out of a lake they hit him on the head with a log and then buried him in a decayed tree lying on the river bank. I know what happened to him but I cannot tell you any more—only that I have his possessions in a suitcase I keep under my bed in my house in São Paulo. Now it is time to go to bed—perhaps Pyuni will take you fishing tomorrow. I sent him to São Paulo to be educated so that he can employ his intelligence, which is considerable."

When I woke up the next morning I saw I was in a dormitory whose windows had no glass in them. The wall was blotchy and when I reached out and prodded it, my finger went straight through the termite-pulped wood. Several Indians were leaning through the windows, grinning and pointing at me.

Orlando and I had breakfast together, after which Pyuni came to collect me. We walked through the jungle and I was pleased to find that there seemed to be no mosquitos about; malaria at that time reached its peak two or three times a year, and created havoc amongst the tribes.

We stepped into a canoe, and Pyuni started to paddle. We reached a sandbank and he held the canoe steady so that I could disembark. "We have many piranhas here; they are not good to eat, but they make good bait. Would you like to see one?"

I told him I would, so he produced an old Duckham oil drum round which he had wound about fifty feet of wire. The hook the wire was attached to also had a small metal spoon behind it, and when Pyuni stood on the sandbank and began to whirl the device round his head in the way a cowboy handles a lasso, the centrifugal force flung the glittering spoon and hook far across the water. There was a splash and the water foamed furiously, as Pyuni pulled a piranha on to the sand. He ran a cutting knife between its serrated teeth, before severing its head and fastening the hook into the carcass. A moment later another much bigger piranha was cannibalistically tearing at piranha meat.

"Good fishing here," said Pyuni, "you don't have to wait long for fish in places where they are always hungry."

I climbed back into the canoe and we made our way back. The river and its lakes cooled the jungle but I was still glad Orlando had lent me a hammock, which Pyuni had slung between two trees in a clearing. I lay back on it and watched a wild turkey explore the undergrowth; it made a hollow, booming noise and shook its wattles like a mayor who has mislaid his after-dinner speech.

Three days later the DC3 air-lifted me out of the Parque Nacional do Xingú and a few days later I was once more in England. On my first day back at the office I knocked at Freddie's door.

"I suppose I get the sack for staying in Brazil for an extra two weeks, Freddie?"

"Dear boy, there's nothing you could do that would make me sack you." He stood up. "Let's go and crack a bottle of wine to celebrate your return, and you can tell me all about it."

CHAPTER TWENTY-SEVEN

One interview that defeated me was with a popular band called The Temperance Seven, which I tried to interview in a concert hall on a small piece of land called Eel Pie Island, tucked into the Thames not far fromTwickenham. During the 1960s Eel Pie hosted most of Brtain's leading pop groups and specialised in providing a venue for The Rolling Stones as they were starting out, as well as Rod Stewart, David Bowie and Eric Clapton.

The Temperance Seven made a hit out of a song called Winchester Cathedral, but I couldn't persuade them to talk about the song, let alone sing it. They were in high spirits, and pranced about like anarchic colts. I should probably have come back another day, but Eel Pie is rather off the beaten track, and I didn't get round to trying to see them again.

I was also only partially successful in interviewing the Goons at a rehearsal of The Goon Show at the BBC's theatre in Lower Regent Street. There was a packed house, and I was sitting next to John Browell, the producer. One joke was greeted by a howl of laughter from the audience and John shook his head negatively and made a mark on the script. "Can't use that," he muttered.

"Why not? The audience loved it."

"Exactly. It loved it because it understood it. That means the general public across the country would probably understand it, which BBC audiences are not supposed to do."

"Does that mean you can only use jokes they won't laugh at?"

"Correct. Well, as we've finished rehearsing, you'd better start work. I don't expect Peter Sellers will cooperate; when he hides behind the piano like that, he doesn't want to talk to anyone. Harry

Secombe's almost always amiable, and Spike's very funny when he's not having a psychological crisis."

John knew what he was talking about. Harry Secombe invited me to his house at Sutton for a film show of a holiday in Africa, when he danced round a crocodile; Peter Sellers continued to behave like a vole crouching in its hole in a river bank, with his arm over his head, and Spike talked rationally about his family.

The rehearsal arrived at its conclusion accompanied by chuckles but no great outburst of mirth, so either John Browell's censorship had worked, the audience was thick, or the second part of the rehearsal hadn't been as funny as the first half.

I wondered if any producer could bring himself to try to tone down Kenny Everett. I never met him, but imagined him as an interviewee being as amenable to control as a one-man Temperance Seven.

There will always be some outstanding individual even the most experienced interviewer would want to meet, but by and large I found there is a limit to the number of times one can ask a formulaic question and receive in return a formulaic answer without eventually becoming bored. The same of course applies to the interviewee, who becomes at least as bored answering the same old questions as the interviewer does asking them.

I have never interviewed anyone in a studio, with the exception of my abortive attempt with Lawrence Durrell. Studio audiences tend to shape interviews by the way they react, just as all audiences shape a performance in the theatre or cabaret. Laughter aroused by comedy is usually a pleasure to listen to and an encouragement to the performer, but not when it's canned.

Current affairs and news interviews where the interviewer is constantly trying to turn the interviewee into a victim often annoy listeners wherever the interview takes place; politicians subjected to this sort of treatment can usually look after themselves, but the audience is seldom willing to tolerate for long the discourtesy of an interviewer who won't let the subject speak.

Another significant influence on interviews outside the studio is background. The interview with Gerald Durrell was far more fun with the voices of articulate birds screeching their versions of serenades at him whilst roars of affection emanated from the black-footed mongooses he had hand-reared, than audience reaction would have been.

An interview I did with Donald Campbell in 1962, shortly before he broke the world land speed record in his 5000 hp car Bluebird took place at an exhibition of record-breaking cars at Goodwood where Bluebird had been taken for brake tests just prior to making its journey to America's Daytona Beach in what turned out to be a successful attempt to break the 400 mph barrier.

Campbell was a slim, highly personable man when I met him, who had spent his life not only emulating his father Sir Malcolm but perhaps—unwillingly—competing with him. Malcolm was aggressively competitive, and was held to have paid little heed to Donald's gentler outlook. His father's character and personality were powerful enough, Donald believed, to bridge the ectoplasmic world of the dead and the living.

"Is it true that you're a spiritualist," I asked him, "and that your father saved your life on two occasions some time after he died?

"When you say spiritualist, you bring to mind a darkened room full of old women holding hands and trying to contact the dead. My interest lies in trying to discover how many Dimensions there are. We know definitely there are three, and Einstein has spoken of a Fourth, namely Time, but nobody knows for sure. As for my father saving my life, I believe his spirit did so twice. Some colleagues and I were in a speed boat—not Bluebird—and heading very fast for a low pier. I had the steering-wheel in my hands and was sure there was plenty of clearance under the pier, when my hands seemed to be wrenched off the wheel and we broadsided and stopped.

"I looked at the pier and saw I had misjudged the height; if we'd held our course our heads would have been torn from our shoulders." He frowned. "It was a strange feeling, because what saved us was loss of control. I wanted to move my hands in one way but I was forced to do the opposite, "as if my hands were being moved by someone else".

Dramatically, Donald Campbell concluded our interview with the insane sound of his Bluebird car's Proteus turbine engines being switched on. They had the whistling thunder of Concorde's, and would have blasted any normal building to rubble if unleashed anywhere nearby.

In complete contrast, I was walking some years later through a quiet Galapagos meadow without a tape recorder when my guide stopped dead with a finger against her lips. "There are two giant tortoises mating just down there. Can you hear? They are moaning in ecstasy." I stood absolutely still and a two-tone cry which certainly sounded ecstatic wafted towards us. She suggested we go down to look, but I refused her offer; I had no wish to be a voyeur at the scene of an act which took place with the same sort of frequency as an eclipse of the sun.

Perhaps one day some Doctor Doolittle will be able to communicate with a giant tortoise in front of a studio audience and discuss her remarkably long period of gestation, and the biological proceedings which preceded it.

CHAPTER TWENTY-EIGHT

Dick Francis invited me to lunch with him at the Reform Club in Pall Mall one day in 1987. Owing to his ambition his career had at times tended more towards turbulence than calm, and he had gone through a cyclonic stage during the previous weeks when he had virtually been driven out of the BBC by Alasdair Milne, the BBC's Director-General since 1981.

Dick's departure had featured in most of the national press, and those of us whose friendship with him had survived the years wondered what he would do next. He had put on a good deal of weight since we had last met, and his complexion had grown as ruddy as a sea-captain's. His second family, which I had never met, was grown up, and Beata's features were amorphous in the mists of history, no doubt to both of us.

When we were sitting down Dick raised his glass. "Let's drink to Alasdair."

"What? I thought you'd been sacked by him only a few days ago!"

"True, but the timing couldn't have been better. I've been invited to take the one job I wanted as much as the BBC Director-Generalship, and the knighthood which automatically goes with it, so my enemies will be livid."

"Good God! What on earth is it?"

"Director-General of the British Council. It involves a satisfactory amount of travel as well. There's going to be a powerful armada of British culture starting to flow into Europe soon—I have, as they say, got many plans for the Council."

"Well, I'm delighted for you." I raised my glass to him. "Here's to Sir Richard Trevor Langford Francis."

"I think it's enough to arouse a satisfying quantity of venom, don't you?"

I laughed. "I don't expect the fangs of the envious will be able to pass much of it on, though. I imagine the British Council can take care of its own."

"Apparently the DG rates as a senior diplomat, so I shall be able to seek shelter in one of our embassies if I need to."

As it turned out Dick was a remarkably good British Council DG, giving that organisation the attention it needed and bringing it up to date during the five years he was given to run it.

In 1992 he died of a stroke, aged only 58. As our close friends are an integral part of our histories they live on; we cannot replace them but if we are lucky we go on meeting people who may become close and offer our lives some sort of illumination.

The actor Charles Gray, so adept at playing villains, was a pub acquaintance. He had a high, snarling voice and was extremely tall and slender. He liked young men and despised girls, with the exception of Ava Gardner, but in my experience she never entered the pub, the Ennismore Arms, just round the corner from Rutland Gate in Central London, although she lived only a few yards away. It was turned to rubble by its owners round about the turn of the millennium before the developers incorporated it into a new building.

One of our regulars was a Geordie porter in a block of flats nearby, who had three pints of John Smith on a daily basis before falling asleep against the cigarette machine at the end of the bar.

Charles came in one evening, bought his usual quadruple pink gin, turned to the unconscious porter and commented: " There isn't much Madame Tussaud could do for you, is there Bob?"

158

On another occasion he shocked my female companion, who wanted to meet him, by completely ignoring her. "Walter, do you know an actress called Viola Tree?"

"I don't think so, Charles."

"Well it doesn't matter a damn whether you do or not, I only mention her because she kept a mongoose in the bathroom." He licked his thin lips. "And you know what mongooses like to eat? I didn't have to worry when I went to pee, though. My fairy godmother forgot to give me an anaconda" He turned away, immaculate in a red check suit, to speak to someone else. My companion looked like someone who has just been electrocuted.

One of the many peers living in Knightsbridge was Lord Ian Rerwick, who refused to take his seat in the House of Lords until £14 million he alleged his father had stolen, was returned to him. As it apparently never was, he remained seatless. He did however frequently regale his friends with Victorian poems and verses from his immense mental warehouse of anthology.

I introduced him to a friend of mine, a corporate banker who had managed to fight off committal proceedings against him for allegedly stealing a lot of money from his bank. "Did you really steal £5 million quid?" I asked after his acquittal.

"£5.3 million, *if* you please."

"Someone I know thinks his father, a bank chairman, has made off with a fortune that belongs to him. I thought you'd be able to give him some tips on how to get it back."

"I'll do my best, for a modest finder's fee." I did introduce them, but the money remained hidden and Ian Rerwick never took his seat.

When I was asked to give the eulogy at the funeral of David Booth, a dear friend of mine who had been a theatrical agent, I recited one of Ian's verses which had made David laugh in hospital, three days before his death. The presiding Canon at the service asked me to read it:

"Have you met my daughter, Sir?

"She cannot hold her water, Sir.

"Every time she laughs she pees

"So do not make her laugh, Sir, please."

John Thaw, the Boulting Brothers, and other clients of David sitting in the front pews, asked me to write the verse down for them. So far as a funeral can be a success, the anonymous Victorian poet had contributed much to it.

CHAPTER TWENTY-NINE

My final reminiscence is of a visit to Patagonia shortly after the start of the millennium.

Alison and I were aboard a cruise ship whose captain informed us each morning over the ship's sound system of matters pertaining to the day: its meteorology, any historical association with the date, our navigational position and so forth.

That morning he had reminded us we could be looking at the same view Darwin had seen from the Beagle, as we were sailing through the Beagle Channel.

We went on deck and looked at our surroundings. Ice lay neat and inert, zebra-striping the black rocks of endless glaciers stretching towards the immense dignity of the Andes. One petrified tree was poised in a permanent triple-armed salute as it stood rigidly above the shore line.

"I wonder if Darwin saw that," Alison remarked.

"No, he did not." The voice was that of a Phillipina woman standing nearby. Her eyes were screwed up against the sunlight, her legs invisible in the thick shadow of a tender, like a pen nib in an ink well. She looked middle-aged, tender and wise; I think she was the sister who ran the ship's hospital.

"You sound pretty positive about that," I put in. "The Captain said the opposite in his remarks just now."

"The Captain said that we were in the Beagle Channel too, but we are not."

"Do you mean to say the captain's not telling the truth?" Alison asked.

"That is the case. We are in a very similar channel to the Beagle. You see, The Beagle takes us to Puerto Arenas, but so much ice and snow have melted that the town is flooded and we would probably capsize if we tried to enter it. Forgive me for telling you the truth. It is difficult sometimes to know whether it is better not to. Some people panic when they are on a ship and the words 'capsize' or 'flood' are spoken. She went inside. In the dstance, high in the hurtfully bright sky, a condor flew towards us like a metaphor for beauty.